PIRATES, SOLDIERS
&
FAT LITTLE GIRLFRIENDS

★ More Classic Texas Sports Quotes ★

PIRATES, SOLDIERS
&
FAT LITTLE
GIRLFRIENDS

ALAN BURTON
illustrations by RICK ATKINSON

ZONE PRESS
Denton, Texas

Pirates, Soldiers & Fat Little Girlfriends
More Classic Texas Sports Quotes
Alan Burton
Illustrated by Rick Atkinson

Published in the United States of America
By Zone Press

www.ZonePress.com

an imprint of
Rogers Publishing and Consulting, Inc.
109 E. Oak, Ste. 500
Denton, Texas 76201

All Illustrations: Rick Atkinson
Design & Layout: Randy Cummings

ISBN: 978-0-9817442-9-2 (13)
0-9817442-9-X (10)

This book is dedicated to the memory of Thomas "Golden" Gentry, a longtime friend and dedicated fan of the Sherman Bearcats.

OTHER BOOKS BY ALAN BURTON

"...til the fat lady sings" Classic Texas Sports Quotes
Texas Tech University Press (1994)

"rave on" Classic Texas Music Quotes
Texas Tech University Press (1996)

Texas High School Hotshots: The Stars Before They Were Stars
Republic of Texas Press (2002)

Dallas Cowboys Quips and Quotes
State House Press (2006)

Table of Contents

Foreword

I currently have two daughters attending Texas Tech. My oldest, Janeen, told me about *Pirates, Soldiers & Fat Little Girlfriends*, by Alan Burton. She said that there was going to be a book signing at Barnes & Noble in Lubbock over the weekend. My wife, Sharon, suggested she pick up one and get it personally signed for me. Janeen and her husband, Mike, came to visit us in Key West shortly thereafter and brought the autographed book with them. My wife read it first and thoroughly enjoyed it, as did I. When contacted to write a foreword for this newly-revised edition, I was more than happy to do so. This new edition includes a new ending ("A Pirate Can Beat A Solider — The Final Chapter") with additional quotes from yours truly.

I've always tried to tell the truth and value honest dialogue. In my press conferences, I seldom began with an opening statement. Instead, I would immediately open it to questions. By being straightforward, you have far less to keep track of, and football gives you plenty to keep track of as it is. When I came to Texas Tech, it was my honor to follow Coach Spike Dykes, who was revered and respected around the country. He has always been supportive of me, and I've appreciated that. My opportunity at Texas Tech was enriched by the character and foundation that Spike had built there.

Pirates, Soldiers & Fat Little Girlfriends is an entertaining oral history of Texas sports without the boring stuff. I really like the variety of the book, different sports, some politically correct quotes and some not. It affirms the stereotype that everything is bigger in Texas, including the sports personalities. Some of the sports legends include Darrell Royal, Bum Phillips, Abe Lemons, Tom Landry, Jimmy Johnson, etc. All of these individuals had their own unique styles—besides winning, they promoted the game with their personalities and quotes. I'm honored to be recognized in the same book and to be quoted alongside so many great and legendary coaches, many that I've admired since I was a child. Out of all of the possibilities, I'm humbled to be chosen to write the foreword.

More than anything else, I want to thank our fans, players and coaches. Together we enjoyed the ten most prosperous years in the history of Texas Tech Football. I will always cherish the years I spent at Tech.

Mike Leach
October, 2010

Author's Note

Back in 1994, *"til the fat lady sings – Classic Texas Sports Quotes"* was published by Texas Tech University Press. That book offered a comprehensive collection of humorous and thought-provoking quips and quotes from around the Lone Star State.

Now, 16 years later, it's time for the sequel to *"fat lady"* with *"Pirates, Soldiers & Fat Little Girlfriends – More Classic Texas Sports Quotes."*

As the title would indicate, *"Pirates, Soldiers & Fat Little Girlfriends"* was greatly inspired by the many colorful quotes of Texas Tech football coach Mike Leach. Or, as of December 30, 2009, *former* Texas Tech coach Mike Leach. For it was on that day – just days before Leach's Red Raiders were to face Michigan State in the Alamo Bowl – that Leach was fired by Tech.

The controversial dismissal enraged many "Team Leach" supporters, with Leach subsequently filing a lawsuit against the University. All of that is now in the hands of the lawyers.

But the soap opera that involved Leach, the Tech administration, Craig and Adam James, and a shed is a story for another book.

Tommy Tuberville was hired as the new Red Raiders coach, and Leach should deservedly return to the coaching ranks, sooner, hopefully, than later.

"Pirates, Soldiers & Fat Little Girlfriends" is a brand new collection of 600 sports quotes from 1995 to the present, with some classic oldies thrown in for good measure. This volume seeks to embrace and preserve the memorable musings of Leach and many others.

Whether you are a Mike Leach fan or not, he did give Texas Tech football a unique national identity, something that the program had been missing for the last *85 years* or so.

Sadly, Leach is one of the few "characters" in the coaching fraternity today (assuming he returns to the coaching ranks). His candid, off-the-wall comments to the media are a breath of fresh air, as opposed to the politically-correct (yawn! – see Mack Brown) mutterings of most coaches. What Leach has to say might make you laugh, might make you mad (see Aggies), or, more than likely, make you scratch your head. But at least you listen to what he has to say.

Last fall, prior to all of the controversy, Leach was on the set of the ESPN studios, discussing his philosophy in dealing with the media.

"I try to be honest," Leach said. "Things have gotten a little too homogenized in this country, and I think people should be allowed to speak their mind. Otherwise, we're going to bore each other to death."

Amen, coach, amen.

Introduction

"Fat little girlfriends."

With those three magical words, Texas Tech football coach Mike Leach earned a place in the mythical "All-Time Sports Quotes Hall of Fame," along with an in-studio appearance on ESPN and immortality in the modern world of You Tube.

So what's the story behind, ahem, the "fat little girlfriends?"

Well, it seems that Leach and his Red Raiders were well on their way to another outstanding season in 2009. After a couple of early season losses to Texas and Houston, the Raiders were back on track with a 5-2 record and a national ranking (21st). Plus, pass-happy Tech had just picked up impressive victories over Kansas State (66-14) and Nebraska (31-10), when the struggling Texas Aggies came to Lubbock. A&M, 3-3 on the season, had recently been whipped by K-State (62-14) and arrived at Jones AT&T Stadium as a decided underdog.

However, the rival Aggies stunned the Red Raiders and their hometown fans to the tune of 52-30. Afterwards, Leach was not at all amused by the result or by his team's lack of focus.

"As coaches, we failed to make our coaching points more compelling than their (the players') fat little girlfriends," Leach told the media. "Fat little girlfriends have some obvious advantages. For one thing, their fat little girlfriends are telling them what they want to hear, which is how great you are and how easy it's going to be."

And Leach didn't stop there:

"As coaches, we have to solve our failure on reaching them, and the players have to listen. And I'm willing to go to fairly amazing lengths to try to make that happen. I don't know if I'll be successful this week or not, but I am going to try and there will be some people inconvenienced, and if it happens to be their fat little girlfriends, too bad."

After a mild public outcry over his comments, Leach offered some background material that seemed to imply that "fat little girlfriends" was merely a figure of speech used to deliver a deeper message:

"I worked with a guy from Louisiana in a camp one time – he used to say at the end of drills – he used to say – 'all right, that was a good job, man. Now you can sit under a tree and eat a fish sandwich with your fat little girlfriend and drink a glass of lemonade.' And it's kind of a metaphor for being too comfortable and being too happy, too complacent, too relaxed. It's not just us, but teams all over the country are symptomatic of that. Because, as a coach, you're outnumbered…I mean, a player comes into your locker room, your meeting, and you've only got so many coaches, and we're telling them one thing and, on the outside, other folks are telling them how great they are. Well, our message is a little tougher to swallow, cause it demands work, effort, and dedication. And then so they want to hear the other message more than they want to hear ours."

Perhaps the comment was even a sly psychological ploy designed to wake up his players and to remind them not to believe their press clippings.

For the record, it seemed to work. Tech rebounded from the Aggie debacle to beat Kansas (42-21) the following week. In fact, the Raiders won three of their last four games to finish 8-4 and earn a berth in the Alamo Bowl.

And all of this was not lost on Tech basketball coach Pat Knight, a good friend of Leach.

After his team started the 2009-10 season with nine straight victories, including a win over 12th-ranked Washington, Knight had these words to say in regard to his players:

"Then they read it (press clippings) and their mom reads it and their dad reads it. That, and their *beautiful* girlfriends. You've got to worry about all that."

"1"

"A Pirate Can Beat A Soldier"

Mike Leach is no ordinary football coach. For starters, he never played college football. On the other hand, he possesses a law degree from Pepperdine University.

Known for his prolific high-scoring passing offense, Leach served as offensive coordinator at four schools, including Kentucky and Oklahoma, before taking over as head coach at Texas Tech in 2000.

Leach's brilliant offensive mind and intellectual prowess, combined with his disheveled appearance, led media-types to refer to the Tech coach as the "Mad Professor," "Mad Genius," "Mad Scientist," "Mad Mike," "Captain Leach," "The Strange One," and "Columbo."

In 10 seasons at Tech (he was abruptly fired in late December 2009), Leach compiled an 84-43 record, making him the winningest football coach in school history. His teams played in a bowl game during each of those seasons and, in addition, led the NCAA in passing yardage on six occasions.

Among numerous highlights was the 2006 Insight Bowl, which saw the Red Raiders overcome a 31-point third-quarter deficit to defeat Minnesota in overtime, 44-41. That victory stands as the biggest comeback in Division I-A bowl history.

In 2008, Leach guided the Red Raiders to a 10-0 start and a No. 2 national ranking on the way to an 11-2 season. He even picked up a couple of national coach-of-the-year awards. Along the way, Leach brought Tech and Lubbock unprecedented national exposure, including three nationally-televised games. On one such telecast, the Red Raiders upset top-ranked Texas on a thrilling last-second TD pass from Graham Harrell to Michael Crabtree. Leach was also the subject of national media interviewers, catching the attention of such heavyweights as *The New York Times*, ESPN, and *60 Minutes*.

Life on the sidelines with Leach was certainly never dull – over the past 10 years, he was responsible for the following, among other things:

— replaced his starting place-kicker with a student who came out of the stands at a game to win a halftime promotional kicking contest;

— changed the first name of his starting quarterback from "Taylor" to a more masculine-sounding "Nick;"

— banned his players from using the social networking site Twitter to discuss team matters;

— appeared in a cameo role on the TV show *Friday Night Lights*;

— offered movie reviews, provided dating advice, and served as a guest weather forecaster on Lubbock television;

— weathered, for a year anyway, a nasty and public contract dispute with University officials;

— expressed his displeasure with a player's academic progress by sending that player to midfield at Jones Stadium with a desk and chair to study. This was after a winter workout that included snow flurries. The player was provided a coat to wear.

Like the late legendary basketball coach Abe Lemons, Leach can be brutally honest in his comments, while not bothering with political correctness. And, like Lemons, frequent Leach targets include his own players, as well as the officiating crews. In fact, after roundly complaining about the officiating in a loss to Texas in 2007, Leach was hit with a record $10,000 fine by the Big 12 conference commissioner.

What makes many of Leach's comments humorous is not so much what he says, but how he says it. His typical delivery is a stammering, monotone voice with a deadpan expression on his face. Looks-wise, Leach resembles country singer Vince Gill and pop singer Michael McDonald. And his dry sense of humor has achieved legendary status among reporters during halftime/post-game interviews as well as during news conferences.

Just for fun, Leach once delivered a hilarious weather forecast on Lubbock television station KAMC:

Leach (forecast): "Now, on Monday, it (map) says bad stuff, serious storms…well, you're going to be dead in 100 years anyway. Live dangerously – I would go opposite of that – that's just too strong, too much… me, personally, expect sun. Go out there and expect sun. Have a good time and if you run into the bad stuff, don't let that hamper your day. Don't be a coward – stay out in it and enjoy the day."

Off the field, Leach developed a friendship with eccentric billionaire Donald Trump. He has also expressed a fascination with studying a variety of off-beat, non-jock subjects, including whales, grizzly bears, Daniel Boone, Winston Churchill, Geronimo, and "pirates."

Leach often exhorts his players by saying, "Your body is your sword — swing your sword." Translation: Don't hesitate.

He even had a life-sized replica of a pirate in his office, which sometimes startled visitors such as the custodian. "My office will be dark," Leach said. "She (custodian) goes to clean the office, and it's got this sensor there where all of a sudden the eyes start flashing – 'Ahoy, matey!'"

After his Red Raiders defeated Texas A&M in College Station in 2006, he told post-game reporters: "Once in a while, a pirate can beat a soldier."

"I think he's popular in the coaching community because he is different. You've got a guy here who's not afraid to do what he wants and doesn't care what anybody thinks. I think sometimes they think he's crazy, but crazy like a fox.'

—— Texas Tech offensive coordinator Sonny Dykes on Leach, 2005

"He's the Columbo of football coaching. That's what he is. Dumb like a fox, and smarter than most. Believe me, he knows exactly what he's doing. He sucks a lot of us right in there, let me tell you that."

—— Minnesota coach Glen Mason on Leach, prior to playing Tech in the Insight Bowl, 2006

"DON'T EVER PLAY TRIVIAL PURSUIT WITH MIKE BECAUSE YOU'LL LOSE. HE HAS AN EXTREMELY QUICK MIND. HE TALKS SLOW, BUT HIS MIND HAS A WEALTH OF FACTS.''

—— Leach's father, Frank

"He's one of those guys who tells a joke that only he gets, you know? Sometimes, he's all business. He's just a different breed of person."

—— Texas Tech defensive end Ardell Duckett, on Leach

"Coach's motivational speeches are always the same. He tells very long stories, and you're never sure what they mean. But he's a genius. When we leave the locker room, we all know that we'll have three receivers wide open every play."

— Texas Tech offensive tackle Daniel Loper, on Leach

"In college, I played rugby. I wasn't great at anything, but I was pretty good at a lot of things. Rugby was just a better

Game for me, but it is not a great game for a coach. There are not the stops where you can make the contributions on strategy."

—— Leach

"The people are incredibly similar. They're very friendly people here. The weather's nicer here. The mountains are shorter here."

—— Leach, on the culture shock of living in Lubbock after growing up in Wyoming

"It's important to have good officiating at all levels, so if that means write your congressman, then you may want to consider that."

—— Leach, after his team was penalized 11 times for 84 yards in a loss

"I was in major league politics for 20 years, and the nastiness of that doesn't hold a candle to this recruiting and rumor business. The evidence is pretty solid that these Internet rumors were coming from advocates of other schools, and we needed to put a stop to it. That's one of the reasons (for the extension)."

—— Texas Tech chancellor John T. Montford, on the speculation surrounding Leach and the extension of the coach's contract, 2000

"OVERCOMING ADVERSITY IS A BIG ITEM IN MY LIFE. THE IDEA OF ACHIEVING AND OVERCOMING SOMETHING DIFFICULT IS SOMETHING I REALLY ADMIRE. EVERYBODY WANTS A CHALLENGE, ESPECIALLY COACHES. IT'S THE MOST VOLATILE PROFESSION OUTSIDE OF ACTING."

—— Leach

"Well, outside of Lubbock, expectations aren't very high. But it's okay, we play in Lubbock a lot this season."

—— Leach, on his team's expectations in 2006

"How come they get to pretend they are soldiers? The thing is, they aren't actually in the military. I ought to have Mike's Pirate School. The freshmen, all they get is the bandanna. When you're a senior, you get the sword and skull and crossbones. For homework, we'll work pirate maneuvers and stuff like that."

—— Leach, on the Texas A&M cadets

"I told him to fix his helmet, which I thought was a pretty good coaching point at the time."

—— Leach, on his advice to quarterback B.J. Symons, when his helmet popped off for the third time in a game against SMU

"THEY WAITED FOR US TO STAND THERE AND WET OUR PANTS, APPARENTLY."

—— Leach, when asked what Colorado did to shut down his team's passing attack

Q: "So, do you think the momentum has switched to your side?"
A: "Oh, I don't know. We haven't played worth a damn." (Then Leach ran away.)

—— Leach's halftime TV interview on the field at the Alamo Bowl, 2001

"HE KINDA DOES THAT LITTLE SKIP; I'M SURE YOU'VE SEEN HIM DO IT. HE DID THE SKIP, AND HE SKIPPED DIFFERENT THAN HE SKIPPED BEFORE."

— Leach, after quarterback B.J. Symons injured his knee after a touchdown celebration during a game with Iowa State

"WELL, WES HAD THE HUGE PUNT RETURN AND I THOUGHT THAT ONCE WE GOT HIM SHOWERED OFF, WE'RE GOING TO HAVE EVERYONE HUG HIM."

—— Leach, when asked about the play of Wes Welker after the Texas Tech-A&M game, 2002

"It's not possible for Nebraska as an institution to criticize anybody for a big score."

—— Leach, responding to criticism that he ran up the score (70-10) against Nebraska, 2004

"We're not tough enough to step up there and play to our ability because all we want to do is talk about what happened against Nebraska. Everybody wanted to coast around and look at the other guy and see what he was going to do. It's just a bunch of sheep looking around staring at one another."

—— Leach, expressing his displeasure with his team after they lost to Texas, 51-21. Two weeks previously, Tech had thrashed Nebraska, 70-10.

"Oh, it was real nice. They let me drink Mountain Dew and watch lots of football, so it was pretty good."

—— Leach,, asked about his stint as a guest on the studio set of the Fox Southwest College Football TV Show

"Any time they get stroked, they want to beam over it like they got an A on their report card, and they're going to get an extra quarter to go buy an ice cream cone."

—— Leach, on his team not responding well to positive media coverage

"THERE'S NOT A MAGIC POTION, HARRY POTTER DIDN'T COME OUT HERE AND CAST A SPELL ON US. WE DIDN'T PLAY GOOD. WE WERE FLAT."

—— Leach, after his 13th-ranked Red Raiders were stunned by Oklahoma State, 24-17, 2005

"I'm not a big milestone guy. It's not like I'm gonna sit in a rocking chair, sip herb tea and ask what's the meaning of life."

—— Leach, after beating Oklahoma for the first time in six tries, 2005

"What they may say has never been one of my fears. It's just so that they avoid distractions of their own. We had a process where we had too many guys aspiring to be team spokesmen."

—— Leach, on limiting the number of players available for media interviews

"I never felt like we played what I would call consistently well the entire game on offense. They (players) were more excited about snorting and blowing snot out of their nose than they were settling in, having a clear mind and doing things they were supposed to do."

—— Leach, after a 30-17 win over Kansas

"THAT'S INEXCUSABLE. IT'S NEARLY A CAPITAL OFFENSE BASED ON THE LEVEL OF STUPIDITY THAT'S INVOLVED IN A FALSE START BY A RECEIVER. A RECEIVER'S NOT SUPPOSED TO LISTEN TO THE COUNT, HE'S SUPPOSED TO BE WATCHING THE FOOTBALL. THE ABILITY TO WATCH A BALL AND SEE IF IT MOVES – I THINK THAT'S PRETTY SIMPLE."

—— Leach, on his receivers being flagged three times for false starts in a 13-10 loss to Alabama in the 2006 Cotton Bowl

"I think this is such a great idea, they should limit both teams to 20 plays, then it would really get them over quickly. Then everybody go out and tailgate. The players and coaches can mingle with the fans and really share in the whole game-day activity."

—— Leach, sarcastically explaining his displeasure at the new NCAA rule designed to speed up play and shorten games, 2006

"TCU deserves some credit, and I'll be nice and politically correct about that. But that was the sorriest offensive effort I have ever seen. Today I coached the worst offense in America, which makes me the worst offensive coach in America."

—— Leach, after a 12-3 loss to TCU, 2006

"WE SAW THE COTTON FIELD ON THE DRIVE FROM THE AIRPORT AND SAID, 'YEP, LUBBOCK, TEXAS, WITH PALM TREES.'"

—— Leach, on playing the Insight Bowl in Tempe, Arizona

"It may be incompetence. It may be bias. I don't know. The level of officiating in this game was a complete travesty. I've been in some games that were poorly officiated, and I've never commented on it in eight years. But something needs to be said, and I'm going to say it. Something's got to change. The thing about it is, last year in this instance I bit my tongue, and I regret it. This whole 'do everything status quo,' and 'oh my gosh, the conference might fine me.' Sometimes it's just the right thing to do, and sometimes things aren't going to change unless somebody stands up and says something. Let me try to keep this as impersonal as possible. But am I condemning the (officiating) crew? Hell yeah, I'm condemning the crew. Unless this can change, the Big 12 Conference needs to take a serious look at having out-of-conference officials officiating the Texas Tech-Texas game and perhaps other games where there is proven a bias by officiating. I think it's disturbing that Austin residents are involved in this (referee resides in Austin). People work too hard, too long, there's too much money invested in these games to allow that. It's (replay system) a sham."

— Leach's comments at a post-game press conference, after a 59-43 loss to Texas in Austin, 2007

"COACH LEACH'S PUBLIC STATEMENTS CALLED INTO QUESTION THE INTEGRITY AND COMPETENCE OF GAME OFFICIALS AND THE CONFERENCE'S OFFICIATING PROGRAM. ACCORDINGLY THE SERIOUSNESS OF THIS VIOLATION WARRANTS A PUBLIC REPRIMAND AND THE LARGEST FINE ISSUED TO DATE BY THE CONFERENCE."

— Big 12 Commissioner Dan Beebe (In accordance with the Big 12 Conference Principles and Standards of Sportsmanship, the Conference issued a public reprimand of Texas Tech University head football coach Mike Leach for his comments following the game against Texas. In addition, the Conference also assessed a $10,000 fine for Leach's post-game remarks and put him on notice that any such future behavior would result in a more serious penalty, including a possible suspension.) 2007

"made my feelings known already, so I don't have a reaction...well, good, we've broken records around here before. we're used to breaking records."
— Leach, reacting to the record fine he received from the Big 12

"Anybody who wants to talk to Graham or Michael Crabtree, you can do it in their natural habitat in Lubbock, Texas. I recommend Love Field because DFW (Airport) can be a confusing mess. Love Field, about every hour, goes to Lubbock, Texas, where we have some great steak places. And we'd love to see you."
— Leach, on not bringing star players Graham Harrell and Michael Crabtree to Big 12 Media Day in Kansas City, 2008

"I wasn't happy with that punt at all. That's why they don't let coaches go armed on the sideline, for that very reason. And I'm not sure having those Texas Rangers nearby is a good idea, either."
— Leach, on a fumbled punt by Tech's Eric Morris

"What he did to get in (the doghouse) is highly classified. It's deeply guarded in the bowels of Texas Tech, and it's guarded by the dogs that you saw on Harry Potter. OK? As far as what he did to get out, just made plays. He just focused on being a great team guy and made plays."
— Leach, on why receiver Lyle Leong had been demoted to the second team, 2008

"It's like Sharon Stone said one time after a movie she did. She said, 'no guts, no glory,' and then if we didn't, I felt like we could get it, and we did."

—— Leach, on gambling on a 4th-and-4 from the Tech 36-yard-line late in the Nebraska game. After completing a long pass on the play, Tech went on to win in overtime, 37-31, Fox Sports post-game interview, 2008

"I just try to focus on what is important now and expedite things. I think that in the world of football, a lot of times there's a temptation to pick up rat droppings when elephant droppings are flying everywhere. So we try to focus on elephant droppings around here."

—— Leach

"FOR ALL I KNOW HE HAD FLIP-FLOPS ON, BUT HE WENT DOWN THERE AND POPPED THE THING IN FRONT OF EVERYBODY. WHAT GOT OUR ATTENTION IS HE DIDN'T TAKE ANY EXTRA STEPS AND IT WENT STRAIGHT UP. IT'S NOT LIKE HE WARMED UP. HE WASN'T UP THERE IN THE STANDS WITH SOME LITTLE KICKING NET AND A REMEDIAL SHOE AND ALL THAT STUFF."

—— Leach, on student Matt Williams, who won a kicking contest during a Tech game, and a few weeks later, was invited to walk on at Tech. He later became the team's starting place-kicker. 2008

"IT WAS DEFINITELY A GOOD WIN, BUT I COACHED A 13-YEAR-OLD ALL-STAR TEAM, AND WE BEAT CHEYENNE (WYOMING) ONE TIME AND I THOUGHT THAT WAS A BIGGER WIN."

—— Leach, on the Red Raiders' 39-33 upset of top-ranked Texas, 2008

"It was a manifestation of a lack of focus."
—— Leach, on why his team was penalized 18 times in a game

"Here's a guy that can talk to you about the European Union and Howard Stern in one conversation. He's that diverse."
—— Kansas coach Mark Mangino, on Leach

"THE THING MOST PEOPLE DON'T UNDERSTAND ABOUT BOB IS WHAT A GREAT GUY HE IS TO WORK FOR. MOST HEAD COACHES LOVE TO TALK. IT'S JUST THEIR NATURE. BUT WITH HIM, IT'S NOT LIKE HE'S MR. CHAIRMAN OF THE BOARD OR ANYTHING. HE'S UNIQUE BECAUSE HE'S A LISTENER. HE'S INTERESTED IN WHAT OTHERS ON THE STAFF HAVE TO OFFER. HE TAUGHT ME THAT. SO I'LL LISTEN – UP TO A POINT. BUT PRETTY SOON, I'LL TELL THEM ALL TO SHUT UP BECAUSE I LIKE TO TALK."
—— Leach, on coaching with Bob Stoops at Oklahoma

"THE BIG 12 CONFERENCE SHOULD HAVE AN EXECUTIVE SESSION TONIGHT AND JUST SAY, 'ARE WE ABOUT THE STUDENT-ATHLETE? ARE WE TRYING TO EDIFY AMERICA AND MAKE THIS A BETTER PLACE? ARE WE ACTUALLY DOING THE PROPER THING AND BALANCING THE DUAL ROLE OF BOTH BEING AN ATHLETE AND BEING A STUDENT?' WHEN THEY DO THAT, I THINK THEY WILL FIND THAT NO ONE'S MORE DESERVING THAN THE RED RAIDERS TO WIN THE BIG 12 SOUTH."
—— Leach, on the controversy surrounding Tech, Texas, and Oklahoma tying for the Big 12 South Conference title. Of the three, Tech had the highest graduation rate. 2008

"Ed didn't like showing up and studying at places I felt like he needed to and like the academic people asked him to. So he can go study out there on the 50-yard line. If somehow he fails to do that, then that'll be the last we ever see of Easy Ed."

—— Leach, on sending receiver Ed Britton out in 30-degree weather to study at Jones Stadium in the off-season. Britton was provided a coat, chair, and desk. The receiver did return for his senior season in 2009, catching 32 passes for three touchdowns.

"Mike Leach has had a huge intellectual influence on the sport already. When you look at a Big 12 football game now, versus 10 years ago, it's a completely different event because everybody is watching Mike Leach's offense. Just wait. God help us if he gets a hold of the sort of athletes they get at places like Texas or Oklahoma or USC. Nobody else will stand a chance."

—— Sports author Michael Lewis, CBS 60 Minutes, 2008

"I hope the next Graham Harrell or Michael Crabtree are sitting in their living room and they are astute, studious guys in addition to being talented. They say, "I know what. The (NFL) game is over but I want to watch 60 Minutes. Oh, Texas Tech on 60 Minutes. That's me." And then they come here. Hopefully, it will turn out that way."

—— Leach, CBS 60 Minutes, 2008

"I think that this is the best job that (Leach) is going to get. Mike's a little different, but we like Mike out here. He'd probably have a more difficult time at some other place where he has to play golf with boosters and stuff. We just want Mike to coach football out here and tell pirate stories."
— Texas Tech chancellor Kent Hance, on the school's contract dispute with Leach, 2009

"If (former Tech quarterback) B.J. (Symons) is a product of the system, then he's not getting any of those touchdown passes and all those yards. That means our coaching staff is. That would also mean we could go down to 7-Eleven and get the clerk behind the counter and let him play quarterback."
— Leach, on criticism of his quarterback "system" in 2003

"MICHAEL CRABTREE HAS BEEN MORE SUCCESSFUL AS A RECEIVER THAN THAT GUY HAS AS A COACH. MICHAEL ISN'T A DIVA. HE'S TOO SHY TO BE LIKE THAT. MY DEFINITION OF A DIVA IS SOMEONE WHO'S LOUD AND SELF-ABSORBED. MICHAEL IS THE FURTHEST THING FROM LOUD THAT I'VE SEEN. LET'S SEE HOW ALL THOSE NON-DIVAS DO UP IN CLEVELAND THIS YEAR."
— Leach, responding to reports that Cleveland Browns officials and coach Eric Mangini referred to former Tech receiver Crabtree as a diva, 2009

"I'm happy for Stephen McGee. The Dallas Cowboys like him more than his coaches at A&M did."

—— Leach, on the Cowboys drafting Texas A&M backup quarterback McGee in the fourth round of the 2009 NFL Draft

"I DON'T UNDERSTAND COACH LEACH'S COMMENTS ABOUT STEPHEN MCGEE. HE WAS NAMED OUR STARTER UNTIL HE GOT INJURED. I'VE ALWAYS BELIEVED IN STEPHEN'S CHARACTER, AND I'VE ALWAYS BELIEVED IN HIS TALENT, AND I ALWAYS WILL. I SEE HIM HAVING AN OUTSTANDING NFL CAREER. COACH LEACH IS IN NO POSITION TO COMMENT ABOUT MY RELATIONSHIP WITH STEPHEN MCGEE."

—— Texas A&M coach Mike Sherman, April 28, 2009

"I'm not one to say that's just Mike being Mike. You're not going to get a free pass with me. I don't get a free pass. I would never comment about any of his guys ... He can make a joke once in awhile and everybody can laugh. But not at our expense."

—— Mike Sherman, April 29, 2009

"There's been far more rhetoric around this than I ever would have expected ... I'm not sorry for what I said. I'm sorry if they feel offended."

—— Leach

"THERE IS NOTHING MIKE LEACH COULD EVER SAY THAT WOULD OFFEND ME. I DO FIND IT UNFORTUNATE, HOWEVER, THAT A COLLEGE COACH FEELS THE NEED TO QUESTION THE HANDLING OF A PLAYER BY A STAFF, PARTICULARLY WITHOUT ANY KNOWLEDGE OF THE FACTS OR THE EXTENT OF A PLAYER'S INJURY. IT IS EQUALLY BOTHERSOME THAT A FOOTBALL COACH WOULD QUESTION THE DRAFT STATUS OF A PLAYER. THIS DOESN'T MAKE ANY SENSE TO ME."

—— Mike Sherman, in a statement released by the A&M sports information office, April 30, 2009

"How can anyone not be shocked that they're offended by this? How is that possible? I mean, they're the ones that keep issuing these official statements. I haven't issued any official statement. I just answer questions when somebody asks me one."

—— Leach, April 30, 2009

"The remarkable thing is, all my life I've never been upset with the Aggies one time. They get upset with me anywhere from every four to six months. However, of all the times they've gotten upset with me, our fans or anything I've ever said, it takes a heck of a detective to find something offensive in what I had to say about the draft."

—— Leach, April 30, 2009

"I've always said that it is truly exciting to play Texas A&M—the quality of coaches they have, the great team and tradition and, above all, the quality of players they have. I've always known A&M had great players. The fact that they have the luxury to put a third- or fourth-round draft pick on the bench, to me, identifies what a truly great team they are. It's an honor for us at Texas Tech to have the opportunity to play them. There are numerous players on our team that will never get a look or play a down in the NFL, so you can imagine how exciting it is for me and them to go play a team the magnitude of Texas A&M and look over there on the bench and see third-and-fourth round draft picks."

—— Leach, April 30, 2009

"THERE'S A PART IN WEDDINGS WHERE ALL OF THE WOMEN ARE RACING AROUND CHANGING THEIR POSITION ON VIRTUALLY EVERY SUBJECT. THEIR MOODS GO UP AND DOWN AND THEY ARE NEVER IN THE MIDDLE. YOU JUST TRY TO DISAPPEAR UNTIL IT'S OVER. AND THEN YOU SHAKE EVERYBODY'S HAND AND THEN PAT THEM ON THE BACK … IT WAS A QUICK, PRACTICAL, WORRY-FREE DEAL. LIKE ME, SHE WANTED A SMALL WEDDING AND THAT WORKED OUT WELL. BECAUSE THE PAYOUTS IN PRESENTS DOESN'T EQUAL THE AGGRAVATION."

—— Leach, on his daughter's wedding

"I like it quite a lot. Heck, I stand the whole game. God forbid that an 18- to 22-year-old athlete should have to go stand and cheer his teammates out there."

—— Leach, on providing less bench seating for reserve players on the sidelines

36

"I think Twitter is stupid, to begin with ... I'm not going to sit around with a bunch of narcissists that want to sit around and type stuff about themselves. We'll put mirrors in some of their lockers if that's necessary, but they don't have to Twitter."

—— Leach, on his policy regarding social networking, 2009

"We had a bunch of receivers just eat, ride and warm up this last week."

—— Leach, on his receivers' poor performance in a loss to Oklahoma State

"I'LL BE INTERESTED TO SEE HOW IT AFFECTS THE ACOUSTICS OF THINGS. I THINK A LOT OF TIMES, THE ACOUSTICS IN STADIUMS ARE MORE IMPORTANT THAN NUMBERS. I THINK THE IDEAL STADIUM IS MADE OUT OF SOLID CONCRETE LIKE THE NEIGHBOR'S BASEMENT SO IT ECHOES LIKE CRAZY."

—— Leach, on the addition of 6,000 seats in the higher levels of Jones AT&T Stadium, 2009

"It's kinda like 'Pulp Fiction,' with women."

—— Leach, on watching the TV show Desperate Housewives

✷ **10** ✷

MOST QUOTABLE
TEXAS SPORTS FIGURES OF ALL-TIME

1. Abe Lemons
2. Darrell Royal
3. Lee Trevino
4. Bum Phillips
5. Spike Dykes
6. Mike Leach
7. Jerry Jones
8. Don Meredith
9. Jimmy Johnson
10. Bill Parcells

"2"

"Dance With Who Brung Us"

There was a time when Darrell K Royal was probably the most popular person in the state of Texas. It was said that governors and senators prayed that Royal wouldn't run against them.

As head football coach at the University of Texas from 1957-76, Royal did it all — winning national championships, conference titles, and bowl games. And he did it with a great deal of class that earned the respect of fans and opponents alike.

To top it all off, Royal was a winner who possessed a charming personality and an ability to keep the press happy with his folksy quips and quotes. No coach was more skilled than Royal at deflecting a tough question and then turning a negative into a positive with a clever, crafty reply.

Early in his coaching career, after a few skirmishes with the press, Royal realized the importance of public relations:

"Public relations has become just as important to a coach's career as the goal line defense," Royal wrote in his 1963 book, *Darrell Royal Talks Football*. "There is more press coverage; it is more wide-spread and more concentrated. Radio and television have added to the coach's exposure. Nowadays, the coach is constantly in the public eye. The ability to deal with these added responsibilities is enviable. It's a phase of coaches' training that has been badly neglected in the past. Were I to advise a young man who knew he was going into coaching, I'd beg him to take college-level courses in public relations, public speaking, and—yes—maybe even journalism."

You have to admire Royal's vision—keep in mind this was written in 1963, light years before the advent of sports talk radio, cable TV sports, and the Internet. For many years, the *Darrell Royal Show* on TV, hosted by Austin personality Cactus Pryor, featured UT highlights and folksy humor. Royal's P.R. skills were indeed put to the test in 1965 when his team suffered three consecutive losses to Arkansas, Rice, and SMU.

"My confidence isn't shaken about our methods of doing things," Royal said. "We're going to stick with what we've been doing. There's an old saying, 'You dance with who brung ya.' We'll keep doing the same things that have worked so well for us through the years."

"Every coach likes those old trained pigs who'll grin and jump right into the slop for him."
—— Royal

"They are like a cockroach. It isn't what he eats or totes off but what he falls into and messes up."
—— Royal, after an upset loss to TCU in 1961

"HE DOESN'T HAVE A LOT OF SPEED, BUT MAYBE ELIZABETH TAYLOR CAN'T SING."
—— Royal, on fullback Harold Philipp

"He looks like he needs worming."

—— Royal, on wispy wide receiver Charles "Cotton" Speyrer

"HE'S QUICK AS A HICCUP."

—— Royal, on quarterback Walter Fondren

"HALSELL IS A ROLLING BALL OF BUTCHER KNIVES."

—— Royal, on linebacker Glen Halsell

"You can call in the dogs and piss on the fire now."

—— Royal, after a game-clenching play

"I was as nervous as a pig in a packing plant."

—— Royal, before a big game

"There's a helluva fight going on out there. Why don't you get in on it?"

—— Royal, in a halftime talk to his players, 1967 Oklahoma game

"BREAKS BALANCE OUT. THE SUN DON'T SHINE ON THE SAME OL' DOG'S REAR END EVERY DAY."

—— Royal

"I've always felt that three things can happen to you whenever you throw the football, and two of them are bad. You can catch the ball. You can throw it incomplete. Or have it intercepted."

—— Royal

"I don't know when I will quit coaching, but I do know I'll end my coaching career at Texas."

—— Royal

"THE GREATEST ASSET MR. BIBLE BROUGHT TO THE UNIVERSITY OF TEXAS WAS RESPECT. HE GAVE THE SCHOOL AND THE FOOTBALL PROGRAM SPECIAL CLASS.''

—— Former Texas kicker-student manager Billy "Rooster" Andrews, on Texas football coach D.X. Bible

"Doak Walker is the most authentic player in football history."

—— Sportswriter Grantland Rice, on the famous SMU running back of the 1940s

"That time was a romantic time. I don't think that will ever happen again. I hope it does, but I think I was just very fortunate to come along at a time when there was a fascination with the heroes of Texas sports."

—— Doak Walker, reflecting on his popularity, 1997

"FOR ALL OF US IN THE FOOTBALL BUSINESS, HE WAS THE ONE—THE BIGGEST ROLE MODEL. HE WAS ONE OF THE BEST FOOTBALL PLAYERS I'VE EVER SEEN. IT WAS A GREAT THRILL JUST TO WATCH HIM PLAY. AND HIS MORALS WERE TREMENDOUS. DOAK WALKER WAS THE ABSOLUTE MODEL FOR WHAT A FOOTBALL PLAYER OUGHT TO BE, BOTH AS A PLAYER AND AS A PERSON."

—— Former Dallas Cowboys coach Tom Landry

"They all wanted another Doak Walker. To my mind, Doak Walker was at one place and the rest of us were at another. They were expecting me to be something I could never be."

— Dallas Cowboys quarterback Don Meredith, reflecting on the pressure while he was at SMU in the late 1950s, 1968

"Today, after watching the SMU Mustangs play with such flair, we reached a decision. We will call our new car the Mustang—because it will be light, like your team; it will be quick, like your team; and it will be sporty, like your team."

— Ford automobile executive Lee Iacocca, talking to the SMU team after the scrappy Mustangs lost to Michigan 27-16 in 1963. The company also considered the names Cougar, Bronco, Cheetah, and Colt.

"People will tell you where they were during the UT-Arkansas game, almost the way people know exactly where they were when they learned President Kennedy had been shot."

— Former Texas quarterback James Street, recalling the 1969 Texas-Arkansas Big Shootout, 1999

"At our football banquet I got a clock that didn't work. At the Columbus, Ohio, dinner I got a plaque with my name spelled wrong. That's what happens when you have a 3-7 season."

— SMU quarterback Chuck Hixson, 1970

"I can run like Unitas and I've got hair like (Y.A.) Tittle."

—— Hixson, on his pro prospects

"PLAYING IN FAYETTEVILLE (ARK.) IS LIKE PARACHUTING INTO RUSSIA."

—— University of Texas defensive coordinator Mike Campbell

"They called me in, and I thought I was going to get a raise. And they fired me. I was sort of hot about that."

—— Alabama coach Gene Stallings, recalling his firing at Texas A&M in 1971, 1995

"I WAS REALLY SORT OF THE ANCHOR OF THE LINE. WHEN I WAS GONE, OUR OFFENSE AVERAGED ONLY 490 YARDS A GAME."

—— Texas Tech center David Dudley, on missing four games due to injury, 1975

"I'm no coach. I'm here to run a $2 million business, the athletic department. I didn't leave 24 years with Merrill Lynch to preside over the death of SMU football. Everybody around here likes to blame the Cowboys, but it doesn't wash. There's plenty enough people to support us both. Dallas is a management town, success-oriented. It won't support mediocrity."

—— SMU athletic director Dick Davis, 1976

"NOW WE'VE GOT A GUY (RON MEYER) WHO CAN COPE WITH DARRELL ROYAL. WE HAVEN'T HAD THAT BEFORE. BUT YOU CAN'T REVERSE 17 YEARS OF DECADENCE OVERNIGHT."

—— Davis, 1976

"I KNOW WHY WE HAD SUCH RECRUITING SUCCESS. WE OUTWORK 'EM. I'M YOUNG. OUR HAIR IS STILL GROWING. WE CAN JIVE WITH THE KIDS, YOU KNOW, DANCE WITH THEM."

—— University of Oklahoma coach Barry Switzer, on OU's five-game winning streak against UT (1971-75)

"Why, those sorry bastards. I don't trust 'em on anything."

—— Darrell Royal to reporters in 1976, after publicly accusing Switzer and his assistants of spying on UT practices

"Playing Texas is like going on a big-game hunt. You have to be prepared for two types though—a rhinoceros (Earl Campbell) and an antelope (Johnny 'Lam' Jones). I didn't know if we had the weapons to stop them both. That Johnny Jones is the fastest football player I've ever seen."

—— Texas Tech defensive coordinator Bill Parcells, after a 31-28 win over Texas in 1976

"We have been an embarrassment to the Southwest Conference. I am ashamed."

—— SMU athletic director Bob Hitch, 1985

"I CAN SEE HOW SOME PEOPLE MIGHT CALL US AN OUTLAW CONFERENCE."

—— Southwest Conference commissioner Fred Jacoby, 1985

"The problem is so many people love this university, and their competitive spirit just got out of hand."

—— SMU coach Bobby Collins

47

"You couldn't pay me to go to an SWC school."
—— Dallas Bryan Adams safety Benny Perry, on overtures from the scandal-plagued SWC, 1987

"I didn't go to Texas because I don't like Texas. I didn't like Fred Akers. I don't like the city of Austin. And I don't like their color of orange. It reminds me of puke."
—— Oklahoma Sooners linebacker Brian "The Boz" Bosworth, an Irving MacArthur graduate

"ROOSEVELT LEAKS WAS THE FIRST SUPERSTAR. HE DID MORE TO KICK DOWN DOORS AND BREAK BARRIERS THAN ANYONE. EARL (CAMPBELL) KNEW HE COULD BE AT TEXAS AND BE A STAR, WHICH BLACKS DIDN'T KNOW UNTIL ROSEY CAME."
—— Royal

"If they don't give him the Heisman Trophy, they ought to melt it down."
—— SMU coach Ron Meyer, on Texas fullback Earl Campbell

"It's like comparing a priest and the Pope when you talk about other runners and Earl."
—— University of Houston coach Bill Yeoman

"Well, I want to puke every time I think about our fans booing a football player and especially one wearing orange. I really think that's a direct response that we get from watching pro ball. People booing. That seems to be the thing to do. But, you know, I think it takes an awfully uncaring,unkind person to act that immature in the stands when some guy's out there laying it on the line for them."

— University of Texas coach Fred Akers, after fans booed UT quarterback Todd Dodge, 1985

"He's not a fullback, he's a Winnebago."

— Texas Tech coach Steve Sloan, on Texas A&M running back George Woodard, who weighed 270 pounds

"WE'RE GONNA WIN SOME OF THEM, BUT WE'RE NOT GOING TO WIN THEM ALL. BOWL GAMES HAVE BEEN UNPREDICTABLE THROUGHOUT HISTORY. YOU'VE GOT TO RECOGNIZE THAT THE OTHER TEAM HAS EARNED ITS PLACE THERE, TOO. WE'RE NOT LIKE THE HARLEM GLOBETROTTERS. WE DON'T TAKE A TRAVELING TEAM ALONG WITH US WHEREVER WE GO."

— Akers, on his poor bowl record

"The pressure of this job is not unlike that of the President of the United States. You see presidents going in looking 50 and coming out looking 70. Hell, Darrell (Royal) looks younger today than he did when he retired in 1976."

— Texas Sports Information Director Bill Little

49

"In Texas, it's a little hard to barbecue on the third level of a parking garage. You just don't get quite the same ambience you would under an oak tree."

—— Texas coach John Mackovic, on the game-day social traditions that differ in the Big 8 and SWC

"I don't want this to sound like a cop-out, but the truth is, I was denying to myself that I was acting differently, trying to act as normal as I could, when, in reality, I was acting differently... It was like I was watching the picture from the outside instead of being from the inside."

—— Mackovic, who said he was suffering post-concussion syndrome after a sideline collision a month earlier, 1994

"I CAN'T SPEND TIME LOOKING BACK. THAT'S WHY JET PILOTS DON'T HAVE ANY REARVIEW MIRRORS."

—— Mackovic, when asked to analyze his team's downfall

"The on-field leadership was very erratic. When a team loses 66-3 against a team (UCLA) it's favored to beat, it shows for whatever reason the team chose to quit on that day. They did that a half dozen times while he was coach and that's unacceptable."

—— University of Texas regent Tom Hicks, on the dismissal of Mackovic, 1997

"I REALLY BELIEVE THAT AT THE TIME I WAS COACHING, I HAD A BETTER CHANCE TO WIN THAN COACHES AT TEXAS DO TODAY. IT WAS A FLOWER IN THE BUD AND JUST GETTING READY TO BLOOM WHEN I GOT THERE. IT WAS A GREAT OPPORTUNITY FOR A YOUNG COACHING STAFF."

—— Former Texas coach Darrell Royal, 1996

"WINNING aT TeXaS IS NOT GOING 6-5. THere are SOMe PLaCeS THaT WILL HOLD ParaDeS FOr YOU IF YOU WIN SIX. BUT NOT aT TeXaS."

—— Former Texas coach Fred Akers, 1997

"Arkansas is a loss to us, but I mean it isn't all that big a loss. Good gosh. They'd only won two championships since Heck was a pup."

—— Baylor coach Grant Teaff, on Arkansas leaving the Southwest Conference

"Look at this place. They treat us like pros here."

—— SMU freshman quarterback Dan Freiburger, after seeing the Mustangs' refurbished locker room, 1989

"SMU got the death penalty. We got the living death penalty. It was the most ridiculous penalty in the history of the world."

—— TCU coach Jim Wacker, after NCAA probation resulted in his team's losing scholarships and revenue and being prohibited from TV and bowl appearances for two years, 1990

"I felt like Jim Bowie and Davy Crockett at the Alamo. They just kept giving us the bayonet."

—— University of Houston coach John Jenkins, on a 45-24 loss to Texas

"FOR SOMEBODY WHO IS REALLY A PRETTY GOOD GUY, JOHN HAS MANAGED TO PISS OFF COACHES ALL OVER THE COUNTRY."

—— Texas A&M coach R.C. Slocum, on Jenkins' tendency to run up the score with his Run-and-Shoot offense

"I said it at Arkansas, and I'll say it now. Their games should not count at all. They got mad then, and they'll probably get mad now. But it isn't fair that their games should count."

—— Rice coach Ken Hatfield, on whether Texas A&M's games should count in the SWC standings (A&M was on NCAA probation at the time), 1994

"If they are on probation, their games should not count. Heck, they wouldn't even let us play."

—— SMU coach Tom Rossley, 1994

"THERE'S NOT ANYBODY, AND HASN'T BEEN FOR 50 YEARS, THAT IS TOTALLY INNOCENT WHEN IT COMES TO TEXAS A&M FOOTBALL. THERE ARE NOT ANY OF THEM THAT, OVER FOOTBALL, THAT WON'T SELL THEIR GRANDMOTHER, THEIR SOUL OR ANYTHING ELSE."

—— Mrs. Warren Gilbert, Jr., wife of a prominent Aggie booster, 1994

"I'd like to play (SMU) because I think we could beat them. And my players feel the same way. If they'd like to play on a Safeway parking lot . . . just give us a date and time."

—— First-year University of North Texas coach Matt Simon, 1994

"I KNOW THEY WERE PLAYING UNDER ADVERSE CONDITIONS, NOT PLAYING WITH THEIR STARTING QUARTERBACK. BUT THEY HAVE SCHOLARSHIP PLAYERS, TOO."

—— UCLA coach Bob Toledo, after his 0-2 team upset 11th-ranked Texas, 66-3, 1997

"RICE GIVES THE SAME NUMBER OF SCHOLARSHIPS AND HAS THE SAME NUMBER OF COACHES WE DO. I'M NEVER SURPRISED WHEN THEY PLAY US A CLOSE GAME."
—— Texas A&M coach R.C. Slocum

"I don't think it takes the Secret Service to figure out that A&M is the team to beat."
—— SMU coach Tom Rossley, at a SWC pre-season luncheon, 1995

"We've been too much of a hot-and-cold team the past few years. When we're bad, a 5A team can beat us."
—— Texas Tech linebacker Zach Thomas, 1995

"It didn't make a difference; I'd rather have been pouring water on the sidelines if that would have helped us win the game."
—— Texas Tech receiver Field Scovell III, on making a reception against USC in a Cotton Bowl loss, 1995

"You have to buy his equipment at Toys R Us."
—— UNT coach Matt Simon, on 5-9, 160-pound freshman kicker Robert Hoffman

"IT WAS LIKE THE ALAMO. THEY WERE COMING OVER THE WALLS."
—— Mike McKinney, chief of staff for Gov. Rick Perry, describing the rowdy section of Texas Tech's Jones Stadium in which he was sitting. McKinney suffered a bloody nose in a post-game incident, and after he blamed Tech officials, it was discovered that an Aggie fan had caused the injury. 2001

"If this one can't get your motor running, you need to change your oil."

—— TCU linebacker coach Charlie Rizzo, on facing Kansas in a nationally-televised game, 1995

"It's exposure for the university; it's exposure for the players. Plus, they pay you a lot of money for playing on Thursday nights."

—— Kansas coach Glen Mason, on meeting TCU in a Thursday night national TV game

"I SHOULDN'T COMMENT, BECAUSE I'LL GET IN TROUBLE. BUT IT MAKES ME WANT TO THROW UP."

—— SMU coach Tom Rossley, on a controversial officiating decision

"Ray Charles could have seen that one."

—— Rossley, when game officials missed a fumble recovery by his team

"I like Tom (Rossley) a lot personally. I like his values and the values he has for his kids...But Tom will be the first to admit that he is in a business where winning is important. We've got to show some improvement in that direction... Tom knows eventually we have to do that."

—— New SMU athletic director Jim Copeland, 1995

"THERE'S BEEN DISAPPOINTMENT AT SMU EVER SINCE (THE NCAA) CAME DOWN ON US. WHAT WE NEED TO HAVE IS A WINNING SEASON. IT WOULDN'T MATTER WHAT LEAGUE WE WERE IN. IF WE WERE IN A LEAGUE WITH RUSSIANS AND CHINESE, IT WOULDN'T MATTER. WE JUST NEED TO WIN."

—— Rossley, on joining the Western Athletic Conference

"I never really liked Kim Helton. He's real wishy-washy."

—— Texas linebacker Tyson King, on Houston coach Kim Helton

"I think pre-med would be tougher (than making his first start against Baylor). But when I'm taking a pre-med test, it's only numbers. Nothing's moving around."

—— Texas quarterback Richard Walton, a pre-med student, on making his first collegiate start, 1995

"I think you've got two very classy groups of kids who are going to get together and knock the snot out of each other."

—— Houston coach Kim Helton, on meeting Rice in the SWC's last game, 1995

"We could play Texas 300 times and we still won't win."

—— New Mexico State football coach Jim Hess, after a 41-7 loss to Texas, 1996

"WE HAVE ABOUT AS MUCH CHANCE AT BEATING TEXAS AS I DO GETTING A DATE WITH SHARON STONE. BUT IF YOU'RE IN HOLLYWOOD, YOU MIGHT AS WELL TRY. AND WE'LL BE IN AUSTIN, SO WE MIGHT AS WELL TRY."

—— Hess

"When Hayden (Fry) was here we were close; we almost knocked the door down. At the time, the Southwest Conference was like a wall, and now with the Southwest Conference gone, it's like the Berlin Wall is down."

—— UNT coach Matt Simon, on the school's efforts to join a big-time conference, 1997

"They clogged our arteries, and then they kicked our tails."

—— Oklahoma State Assistant Sports Information Director Mike Strauss, who enjoyed the Mexican food buffet in the Royal-Memorial Stadium press box more than Texas' 71-14 rout of the Cowboys, 1996

"WE'RE NOT A VERY GOOD FOOTBALL TEAM. THAT'S THE BOTTOM LINE. NOW THAT'S MY FAULT. THAT HAS NOTHING TO DO WITH THE PLAYERS."

—— Baylor coach Chuck Reedy, after his 4-6 Bears were upset by Missouri, 1996

"If the truth be told, there is not a lot of difference between an Aggie and a Cheesehead."

—— Texas A&M assistant football coach Mike Sherman, after leaving A&M to become an assistant with the Green Bay Packers, 1997

"I MUST HAVE BEEN AN IDIOT TO THINK I COULD COME IN HERE AND CHANGE WHAT THEY'VE BEEN DOING FOR NINE YEARS IN TWO WEEKS. THIS IS THE THIRD TIME I'VE DONE THIS (TAKEN OVER A LOSING PROGRAM). I KNEW IT WOULD TAKE YEARS, NOT WEEKS."

—— First-year SMU coach Mike Cavan, after a 46-16 loss to Navy, 1997

"RIGHT NOW, WE'RE PROBABLY, I THINK, ABOUT AS BAD A FOOTBALL TEAM AS THERE IS IN AMERICA."

—— Baylor coach Dave Roberts, after his 1-3 Bears lost to Texas Tech, 1997

"Last year, we were inept. We're not very good right now, but we're not inept."

—— Roberts, after an opening-season loss to Oregon State in 1998

"I don't want to sound disrespectful of the Cotton Bowl, but this will be the greatest day of my life to say that's the last time we're going down there. We want to get back on campus. I don't want to take anything away from Doak Walker and the day when that was the only game in town, but we need to get back on campus."

—— SMU coach Mike Cavan, on leaving the Cotton Bowl to play in the new Gerald J. Ford Stadium on campus, 1999

"If I helped inspire some black kids along the way, that would make me happy. But I always just wanted to be a quarterback, not a black quarterback."

—— University of Texas quarterback James Brown, 1997

"MACK ALWAYS WANTED A SHOT AT A PROGRAM WITH TRADITION. HE WANTS TO BE AT A PLACE WHERE FOOTBALL'S NO. 1, WHERE THE FOOTBALL STADIUM IS THE PLACE TO BE ON SATURDAY. THE BAND, BEVO, THE POMP AND CEREMONY, THE STEERS ON THE HELMET — HE LOVES ALL THAT STUFF."

—— University of North Carolina professor Dick Coop, a close friend of North Carolina coach Mack Brown, on Brown taking the Texas job, 1997

"Even Betty Crocker burns a cake every now and then."

—— Texas Tech's popular quarterback Billy Joe Tolliver, after struggling and being booed and benched at home

57

"He has the magic that people saw in a young Darrell Royal."

—— UT regent and football search committee member Tom Hicks, on new UT coach Mack Brown

"I hope they get the lights fixed here. Maybe they can call the president (Clinton) and get him to send some money down. It's a natural disaster."

—— SMU coach Mike Cavan, after a power failure at War Memorial Stadium in Arkansas

"FROM EVERYTHING I CAN TELL, HE'S A REAL CLASS GUY. I KNOW SOME PEOPLE DON'T APPROVE OF HIS HAIR (DREADLOCKS). BUT SOME PEOPLE PROBABLY DON'T APPROVE OF MY HAIR."

—— Texas A&M coach R.C. Slocum, on Texas running back Rickey Williams

"This isn't my first rodeo. I've been in big games before. In the spring, I asked people if they wanted to beat Texas A&M or Oklahoma more. They said 'Yes.' "

—— First-year Texas coach Mack Brown, on the eve of his first Texas-Texas A&M clash

"THEY DO NOT WANT TO PLAY US. PERIOD. THEY HAVE NOTHING TO GAIN AND EVERYTHING TO LOSE. I'M SURE THEY LOOKED AT SOME OF THE TAPES AND REALIZED WE HAVE A CHANCE TO WIN. I'VE LIVED IN TEXAS FOR FOUR OR FIVE YEARS, AND I'VE NEVER KNOWN A TEXAN TO BACK DOWN FROM A FIGHT BEFORE. I GUESS THEIR COACH ISN'T FROM TEXAS."

—— Then-Hawaii coach June Jones, on Texas and coach Mack Brown being released from a contract to play his team. Hawaii went 8-4 in 1999 after an 0-10 record in 1998.

"YOU FEEL LIKE YOUR GIRLFRIEND JUST LEFT YOU AND YOU DON'T KNOW WHY."

—— Texas quarterback James Brown, describing his feeling after a 24-24 tie with OU, 1995

"My first taste of Texas was when I went downtown during Texas-OU weekend. I was a freshman. I saw a priest from my high school drunk in the gutter. I almost got beat up three or four times because I didn't know if I was supposed to say I was for Texas or OU. I went into Jack Ruby's strip club and I realized I wasn't in the North anymore. It was cool."

—— Sony Pictures Classics co-president Tom Bernard, on moving from New Jersey to Dallas, 2005

"When little old ladies are giving you the bird, that's when I knew there was some bad blood in this game."

—— Texas cornerback Roderick Babers, recalling the fact that when he walked on the field, elderly female OU fans in the stands made obscene gestures

"The only way I know to describe the feeling you have before the game is that when you walk onto the field, there is a force field of electricity. You actually visualize streams of electrical current coming off the field. You feel like you're walking a foot off the ground."

—— Texas coach David McWilliams, on the Texas-OU game

"THE RAIN CAME DOWN SO HARD, AND THE COTTON BOWL ASTROTURF WAS SO SLICK THAT PLAYERS COULDN'T STAND UP IN THE FIRST HALF. THERE WERE ALSO A COUPLE QUESTIONABLE CALLS IN THAT GAME. CAN I CRITICIZE OFFICIATING IN A GAME THAT'S 10 YEARS OLD WITHOUT GETTING FINED?"

—— Texas coach Mack Brown, recalling the 1984 UT-OU game in which Brown was the OU offensive coordinator

"I can proudly say that I never lost to Texas. Yes, we tied one game, but it's still not a loss. But I can guarantee everyone on that field knew who won that game. And that includes Fred Akers."

—— Oklahoma linebacker Brian "The Boz" Bosworth, after the OU-Texas game ended in a 15-15 tie in 1984

"I shouldn't have done that. There's no need to talk on the field. I should leave the talking to people like Jerry Springer. I had to apologize for that last year."

—— Texas quarterback Major Applewhite, when he got into an altercation with OU players and fans in the 1999 game

"That was a pretty tough one to swallow. It wasn't a shootout. We just got shot."

—— Texas A&M coach R.C. Slocum, after a 51-6 loss to Oklahoma, 1999

"I just fell in love with A&M. Texas just wasn't my style. You got people in Austin with green hair. One guy had a chain from his nose to his belt loop."

—— Texas A&M linebacker Brian Gamble, 1999

"Earl Campbell was the Tyler Rose. I'd like to be known as the Tyler Thorn."

—— Baylor cornerback Gary Baxter, 2001

"SPEAK NO EVIL. IF YOU'RE IN THE BARBERSHOP OR THE COFFEE SHOP, DON'T BAD-MOUTH BAYLOR FOOTBALL. THAT PERSON HEARING WHAT YOU SAY MIGHT BE THE FATHER OR MOTHER OF A YOUNG MAN INTERESTED IN PLAYING AT BAYLOR."

—— Baylor football coach Guy Morriss

"I'll go down as the coach who lost one quarterback to a rock band and one quarterback to Ernst & Young."

—— SMU coach Phil Bennett, on two of his quarterbacks who departed prior to the 2002 season to pursue careers in music and accounting

"That program is a joke, and it will always remain that way. It's really sad, pitiful. You can't blame the players. The coaches are where it starts."

—— Former SMU star Eric Dickerson, on the struggling Mustang football team, 2004

"For Eric Dickerson to sit back in California and complain about things, to me, is irresponsible. He is not trying to help us."

—— SMU athletic director Jim Copeland, responding to Dickerson's comments

"The Wishbone offense, in my opinion, is the soundest offense that's ever been put together. It would be just as successful today as it has been."

—— Former coach and wishbone innovator Emory Bellard, 2005

"THANKS TO VINCE AND THE GUYS, I KNOW WHO FIFTY — I MEAN FITTY — CENT IS."

— Texas coach Mack Brown, who listened to hip-hop music on the advice of quarterback Vince Young, 2005

"Just playing close is like showering with your sister."

— Baylor coach Guy Morriss, after a 16-13 overtime loss to Texas A&M

"We sent them Davy Crockett. We sent them Sam Houston. And then we sent them Mack Brown."

— Cookeville, Tenn., optometrist Ralph Mullins, on Tennessee's contributions to Texas. UT coach Mack Brown is from Cookeville.

"In my lifetime, I've not seen one player affect an entire program the way Vince Young has."

— ESPN college football analyst Kirk Herbstreit, on Texas quarterback Vince Young, 2006

"FORGET WHAT HE'S DOING ON THE FIELD. WATCH HIM ON THE SIDELINES. THE WAY HE TALKS TO HIS TEAMMATES, AND THE WAY THEY REACT TO HIM. WATCH THE WAY HE ASKS FOR THE CROWD TO GET MORE INVOLVED. VINCE YOUNG HAS LIFTED UP AN ENTIRE UNIVERSITY, IN MANY WAYS, WITH LEADERSHIP SKILLS THAT ARE GOD-GIVEN."

— Former Texas quarterback James Street, 2006

"My professional opinion, as Secretary of Education, is that Vince Young definitely needs to stay in school."

— Texas native Margaret Spellings, 2006

"Coach (Darrell) Royal gave me some advice a long time ago. He said when you have a really successful year, 'Don't get caught sitting in the shade.' What he meant was, don't sit back and rest on your success, build on it."

— Texas football coach Mack Brown, after winning the 2005 national championship and then signing an outstanding recruiting class

"I get tired of being treated like a stepchild in this state and in this town and my kids do too. We've been waiting for this one for a long time. We may not get the top 100 (recruits), but we got pretty dang good players."

— TCU coach Gary Patterson, after a 12-3 win over Texas Tech

"There was probably a lot of luck involved in that. That first pick - no offense to my mom - but she probably could have caught that."

— Texas Tech linebacker Brock Stratton, after intercepting two passes against Iowa State, 2006

"When I wake up in the morning, I have no regrets. I brush my teeth, I look in the mirror, I'm an Aggie."

— Texas A&M tight end Martellus Bennett, when asked if he regretted picking A&M over a host of other schools, 2006

"That's not what I said; my exact statement was, 'I wish the attitude at our stadium would be like the attitude was when we had the tornado here.' "

—— Former Texas Tech football coach Jim Carlen, 2006 (In the early 1970s, Carlen was accused of telling the audience at his weekly luncheon that Lubbock needed to be hit by another tornado.)

"IT'S LIKE HAVING A NEW GIRLFRIEND; YOU'RE REAL EXCITED ABOUT WHAT'S GOING ON AND WHAT YOU'RE GOING TO DO. COACH BRILES HAS BROUGHT A NEW KIND OF ATTITUDE. HE'S A DIFFERENT KIND OF GUY. HE'S A WEST TEXAS GUY, TALKS 10 MILES PER HOUR AND MOVES REAL FAST. HE DON'T SAY THINGS TWICE."

—— Baylor offensive tackle Jason Smith, on new Baylor coach Art Briles, 2008

"We had to take a big step today. It didn't matter if we were playing Army, Navy, Air Force, Marines, or the Dallas Cowboys. We had to take a big step."

—— Texas A&M coach Mike Sherman, after a 21-17 win over Army, 2008

"...calling attention to one's self."

—— Referee Jack Childress, explaining on the field through his microphone why Mississippi was penalized for excessive celebration at the 2010 Cotton Bowl game

✯ 10 ✯

BEST DESCRIPTIONS
BY HUMBLE/ENCO/EXXON FOOTBALL BROADCASTERS

1. *"The Blond Bomber Bobby Layne fakes a pitch to Byron Gillory, spins on a top and says, here you take it Tommy, as he hands off to Tommy Landry, who bucks into the Pony line. But, there again, doing yeoman service is Dandy Dick McKissack, who says, whoa there Tommy, and holds him for a two-yard gain."*

—— Kern Tips

2. *"Walker tries thunder at right guard but Mr. Watson says, oh, no you don't, and puts a cork in his bottle for a gain of one."*

—— Tips

3. *"There was a malfunction at the junction."*

—— Tips, describing a fumbled exchange

4. *"Let's hear from the orchestra pit."*

—— Connie Alexander, referring to the playing of a school song

5. *"He was horse-collared down."*

—— Alexander

6. *"Flags fell like autumn leaves."*

—— Alexander, on several penalty flags thrown on a play

7. *"He tried to deliver the mail, but someone was reading the letter."*

—— Tips, describing a big hit

8. *"Lam (Jones) runs into a Steve Sloan cyclone — the Raiders were attacking like rabid rhinos."*

—— Alexander, broadcasting a Texas-Texas Tech game

9. *"Walter Fondren skips across the daisies into Royal soil."*

—— Tips, describing a touchdown run

10. *"Allison bows under and barks out the signals."*

—— Jack Dale

(tie)

"He had to peel it and eat it that time."

—— Tips, on a quarterback sack

"3"

"Dogs Chasing Cars and Pros Putting for Pars"

Lee Buck Trevino brought two things to the Professional Golfers Association (PGA) Tour in the late 1960s – an unorthodox swing that produced a pronounced fade and a wise-cracking, happy-go-lucky attitude.

Trevino was a true "rags to riches" story, having overcome a poverty-filled childhood to ascend the heights of the professional golf world in 1968, when he won the U.S. Open. The self-taught player from Dallas would go on to record a brilliant career, earning six major championships, 29 total regular tour victories, and 29 senior tour wins.

Nicknamed "The Merry Mex" and "Super Mex," Trevino delighted galleries with his constant bantering and chattering throughout his round. As a result, the stuffy country club world of professional golf would never be the same.

Traditionally, pro golfers were a quiet, serious lot, with the likes of Ben Hogan so focused that rarely were any words spoken during competition. Trevino was just the opposite, curing his nervousness by talking to his playing partners (some of whom didn't appreciate the conversation) and telling jokes to the crowd. He quickly became a fan favorite and attracted huge galleries wherever he played. In time, his popularity (and game) rivaled that of fellow competitors Arnold Palmer and Jack Nicklaus.

Trevino was also a favorite of the press, offering up colorful quotes as well as stories from his past.

On the first tee of their playoff for the 1971 U.S. Open Championship, Trevino playfully tossed a rubber snake at stern opponent Nicklaus. Everybody laughed, and Trevino went on to win the playoff, shooting a 68 to Nicklaus' 71 at the storied Merion Golf Club.

When asked about the status of the rubber snake in 2007, Trevino replied: "One of my ex-wives has that now. I think it was the second one. I really can't remember."

"I'm gonna buy the Alamo and give it back to Mexico."
—— Trevino, when asked what he was going to do with the $30,000 first prize at the 1968 U.S. Open

"THERE ARE 16 BIRDIE HOLES HERE, BUT THERE ARE 18 BOGEY HOLES. I'LL EAT ALL THE CACTUS AROUND EL PASO IF ANYBODY BREAKS 280."
—— Trevino, on the 1971 U.S. Open at Merion, which he won in a playoff with Jack Nicklaus

"I played 15 good holes and three like Happy Gilmore."
—— Trevino, whose double bogey and bogey knocked him out of a tie for a tournament lead

"MY WIFE'S GOT A BROKEN WRIST, WE'VE GOT A 10-WEEK-OLD BABY, AND OUR DOG'S PREGNANT. I CAME OUT HERE TO REST."
—— Trevino, at the 1969 Byron Nelson Golf Classic

"THERE ARE TWO THINGS THAT WON'T LAST LONG IN THIS WORLD, AND THAT'S DOGS CHASING CARS AND PROS PUTTING FOR PARS."
—— Trevino

"It's just not my kind of course. With my game, I can't play there. They can invite me all they want, but I'm not going there anymore."

— Trevino, on refusing an invitation to play in the Masters

"He said he didn't think he could play this type of golf course. Apparently, we have a better opinion of his game than he does. We think he is skillful enough to play any type of course."

— Masters tournament chairman Clifford Roberts, on Trevino's absence

"It's one of those years. Jimmy Carter had four of 'em, so I don't feel so bad."

— Trevino, on having a bad year on tour

"WHAT'S OVER THERE? A NUDIST COLONY?"

— Trevino, after his three playing partners drove into the woods

"How do you do, Mr. Prime Minister — ever shake hands with a Mexican before?"

— Trevino, on meeting British Prime Minister Edward Heath

"Lee Trevino doesn't want to talk about his back operation. That's all behind him."

— CBS sportscaster Don Criqui

"HOGAN IS THE HARDEST WORKER I'VE EVER SEEN, NOT ONLY IN GOLF BUT IN ANY OTHER SPORT."

— Hall of Fame golfer Bobby Jones, on Ben Hogan

"I'd have to be Houdini to win now."

—— Ben Hogan, on trailing by five shots through 36 holes of the 1951 U.S. Open. He came back to win.

"I'M GLAD I BROUGHT THIS COURSE, THIS MONSTER, TO ITS KNEES."

—— Hogan, after winning the 1951 U.S. Open at demanding Oakland Hills

"I DON'T EVER EXPECT TO QUIT TOURNAMENT GOLF AS LONG AS I LIVE. I'M A PRO GOLFER. THAT'S MY BUSINESS. I GUESS I'LL PLAY GOLF AS LONG AS I CAN DRAG A LEG OUT THERE."

—— Hogan

"He had the sculpted legs of a running back. Like Doak Walker. That's where he got his power. I realized that all great golfers are built with legs like that."

—— Author Dan Jenkins, on Hogan

"If a fellow misses from 40 feet, he grimaces and agonizes like a cowboy struck in the heart by an Indian's arrow."

—— Hogan, on today's golfers, 1975

"Tommy Bolt's putter has spent more time in the air than Lindbergh."

—— Pro golfer Jimmy Demaret, on hot-tempered pro Tommy Bolt

70

"It (golf) was wimp stuff when I was a kid. In west Texas, in the late 1950s, you were either a football player or you were a cowboy or you weren't nothing. Golf was really not considered a sport for real men."
—— Entertainer Mac Davis

"I'M STILL UNDECIDED ABOUT MY FUTURE. PRO GOLF IS A PRETTY TOUGH GRIND. IT TAKES A LOT OF HARD WORK AND THE PRESSURE IS TERRIFIC."
—— Air Force Lt. Miller Barber, an ace amateur golfer in the 1950s, debating whether to turn pro (Barber did so in 1958 and went on to win 35 tournaments and several million dollars). 1956

"I'm no star. Those others are in a different class. Maybe my capabilities are equal, but I never associate myself with Palmer and Nicklaus and them. They've won a passel of tournaments. I've won one. I may never win again, but no matter how many more I win, I won't be like them."
—— Pro golfer Orville Moody, winner of the 1969 U.S. Open, his only PGA Tour victory, 1970

"That dog face can drive a ball through a hole in a doughnut at two hundred fifty yards."
—— Lee Trevino, on the driving accuracy of fellow competitor Orville Moody

"CRENSHAW IS A SUPERSTAR ALREADY, ONE OF THE TOP 10 PLAYERS IN THE WORLD, AMATEUR OR PRO. I THINK HE'LL BE BETTER THAN JACK NICKLAUS WHEN HE GETS ON THE TOUR."
—— University of Houston golf coach Dave Williams, on UT golfer Ben Crenshaw in the 1970s

"He's got the best grip, the best setup and best swing I've ever seen. Besides that, he's nice."

—— Trevino, on Crenshaw, 1974

"I personally think 'Gentle Ben' might be a misnomer. I can be very competitive in sports. I think players I've played with are aware of that."

—— Ben Crenshaw, talking about his nickname, after being named Ryder Cup captain for 1999

"I don't look like someone who should be a star. I'm not tall, I wear thick glasses, I'm kind of pasty-faced, and I don't hit the ball nine miles."

—— Pro golfer Tom Kite

"This course (Augusta National) can make you look like a monkey, and it made me look like one today. I just couldn't get the motor cranking."

—— Defending Masters champion Crenshaw, after an opening round 77 at the 1996 Masters

"We don't pretend to be the U.S. Open. We're more fun than that."

—— Bob Massad of the Salesmanship Club, sponsors of the GTE Byron Nelson Golf Tournament, 1996

"You could be dead and win that."

—— Senior pro golfer Charles Coody, on his meager winnings of $43,000 in his first 13 tournaments in 1996

"David thought I needed to change my setup and my take-away and my backswing and my position at the top and my downswing and my follow-through. But he said I could still play right-handed."

—— Pro golfer Brad Bryant, on swing changes suggested by teacher David Leadbetter, 1996

"NEVER BET WITH ANYONE WHO HAS A DEEP TAN, SQUINTY EYES, AND A ONE-IRON IN HIS BAG."

—— Pro golfer Dave Marr

"Keep your head up. Everything in the world with its head down gets eaten. Chickens, hogs, cows. Every time you see a leopard, his head is up, isn't it? You don't see any leopards getting eaten, do you? No gloomy guy dragging around looking at his shoe tops ever won anything worth winning."

—— Golf legend Jack Burke, Jr.'s advice on attitude to touring pro Steve Elkington, 1996

"I really believe that a lot of golf tournaments have been lost because of a lack of endorphins. You might think that's a silly statement. But you want to get endorphins in your bloodstream, you crack a smile. You find a way to smile, and good things happen."

—— Pro golfer David Ogrin, after winning the 1996 La Cantera Texas Open, his first win in 406 PGA events

"CAN YOU IMAGINE MOVING FROM LONDON TO FARMERS BRANCH? I DIDN'T BELIEVE THEY HAD REAL ROADS AND CEMENT OUT THERE."

—— Pro golfer Andrew Magee, on being born overseas and then moving to Farmers Branch, Texas, 1994

"The boy has more rhythm than Gene Kelly and Fred Astaire put together. And he putts better than both of them, too."
—— Pro golfer Brad Bryant, on fellow competitor Bruce Lietzke, 1994

"I SAW SOME LIGHT AT THE END OF THE TUNNEL. I JUST HOPE IT'S NOT A TRAIN."
—— Pro golfer J.C. Anderson, in trying to break a slump, 1995

"YOU PLAY TO GET YOURSELF INTO SITUATIONS WHERE YOU'RE ABOUT TO THROW UP ON YOURSELF."
—— Pro golfer Brandel Chamblee, after his first tour victory, on paying your dues, 1998

"At so many places, golf is just an interruption from a wedding, from a game of cards or from a cheeseburger. Too many (country) clubs try to solve all of a family's social problems."
—— Jack Burke, Jr., owner of Champions Golf Club in Houston, on his club's emphasis on golf, 1996

"I like the Texas golf courses, the Texas people and the Texas money."
—— Argentina pro golfer Roberto DeVicenzo, after teaming with Rod Funseth to win the 1983 Legends of Golf and $50,000

"... Texas is a golf mecca. People understand golf in Texas probably better, and they play golf with a passion in Texas unlike, I think, anywhere else in the United States. You've got golfers playing in cowboy boots and jeans. They love the game there."
—— Pro golfer Tom Watson, 1999

"IT'S KIND OF LIKE TEXAS IN THE OLD SOUTHWEST CONFERENCE. YOU KNEW WHO WAS GOING TO WIN BEFORE THE GAME. IT'S CERTAINLY FUN WHEN YOU'RE PULLING FOR TEXAS, BUT IT'S NOT REAL EXCITING FOR EVERYBODY ELSE."

—— Tom Kite, on the dominance of Tiger Woods, 2000

"I remember in fifth grade, I read a book about him. I idolized him. He raced cars, and he had a very brash kind of story. A.J.'s going to tell you what he's thinking. He may not always tell the camera what it wants to hear, but he is a true living legend."

—— Race car driver Greg Ray, on legendary driver A.J. Foyt, 1999

"A.J. Foyt is the greatest driver that I ever knew. The best all-around. He could drive anything, anywhere, anytime. Won in about everything he ever sat down in."

—— NASCAR racer Junior Johnson, 1991

"A.J. WASN'T THE BEST DRIVER I EVER SAW, BUT HE HAD MORE WILL TO WIN THAN ANYONE ELSE."

—— Race car driver Parnelli Jones, on A.J. Foyt, 1998

"The lighting will have to be outstanding because a shadow can create problems. At those speeds, you can't come out of a corner and not know where a wall is because of a shadow. Depth perception is a problem. So are bugs. We'll get wasted by those big Texas bugs. But other than that, I think it'll be totally cool."

—— Indy Racing League driver Johnny O'Connell, on what he expected when the Texas Motor Speedway hosted the first night-time Indy car race, 1996

"WHEN I WAS GROWING UP IN TEXAS, RACING WASN'T VERY POPULAR. I CAN REMEMBER RACING AT TEXAS WORLD SPEEDWAY IN COLLEGE STATION AND THEY HAD A COUPLE OF RACES THAT PROBABLY DREW 20,000, 25,000 PEOPLE. NOW THE SPORT'S GROWN ENOUGH TO ALLOW US TO RACE IN OUR HOME STATE, AND THAT'S SPECIAL."

— Race car driver Terry Labonte, 2000

"YOU CAN'T TAKE A SPORT BASED ON WHAT IT LOOKS LIKE ON TELEVISION. DRAG RACING IS A SENSORY SPORT. IT'S THE SMELL, THE FEEL AND THE SOUND. IT'S THE VIBRATION."

— Billy Meyer, Texas Motorplex Speedway owner, 1997

"Comparing what most people grew up thinking about drag racing and what it is today, is as far apart as your 6-year-old's flag football and the NFL."

— Meyer

"History doesn't mean anything in football; history means something in boxing."

— Dallas Cowboys coach Bill Parcells

"I was only knocked down once. It was by Stan Hayward in Philly in 1964 ... I had just gotten married five days before. I was still on my honeymoon. Those kind of things happen when you are young and in love."

— 60-year-old retired boxer Curtis Cokes, recalling his 80-bout career, 1997

"He's a better technical fighter now than as a kid. He was a mean sucker then. He was so mean, German shepherd dogs were afraid of him."

—— Boxing manager Angelo Dundee, on George Foreman, 1994

"I LOVE ALL THREE EVENTS. I'VE WORKED HARD AT 'EM MY WHOLE LIFE. I NEVER WANTED TO BE A BULL RIDER OR A BRONC RIDER. I WANTED TO BE A COWBOY."

—— Rodeo cowboy Ty Murray, on the bareback, saddle bronc, and bull riding rodeo events, 1990

"In this sport, Ty Murray is just it. He's the Bo Jackson of rodeo, the greatest cowboy I've ever seen perform."

—— Fellow rodeo competitor Tuff Hedeman

"There's no possible way Brett Hull can do anything in 11 minutes."

—— Dallas Stars hockey player Brett Hull, complaining about a lack of playing time, 1998

"I LIKE ANY SPORT WHERE YOU CAN DRINK AND EAT WHILE YOU'RE COMPETING, AND BOWLING'S ONE OF 'EM."

—— Dallas sportscaster Dale Hansen

⭐ **10** ⭐

LEAST QUOTABLE
TEXAS SPORTS FIGURES OF ALL-TIME

1. **Duane Thomas**
2. **Marion Barber**
3. **Wade Phillips**
4. **Alex Johnson**
5. **Bobby Collins**
6. **Jerry Moore**
7. **Gerald Myers**
8. **F.A. Dry**
9. **Ed Biles**
10. **Gene Iba/Moe Iba (tie)**

"4"

"Rice and Academic Challenges"

In 1959, 21-year-old William Taylor "Spike" Dykes landed his first coaching job at Eastland High School. Dykes earned a salary of $3,280 while serving as assistant football coach, head basketball coach, tennis coach, golf coach, and World History-American History-Texas History-English I teacher.

From those humble beginnings, Dykes persevered, working his way up the high school and collegiate ranks before eventually landing the head football coaching position at Texas Tech in 1987. Dykes enjoyed success in his hometown of Lubbock, guiding the Red Raiders to an 82-67-1 record and seven bowl games in 13 seasons.

In dealing with the media, Dykes revealed a down-home wit and honest approach to the game. The popular west Texan also earned a great deal of respect for defending his players against criticism, preferring any blame be directed toward him.

But, for many, Dykes will always be the stereotypical Texas high school football coach: the slightly overweight guy with a whistle around his neck who speaks in a country drawl in history class. Dykes looked as if he were perfect for the role of coach Herman Popper in the 1970 movie classic, *The Last Picture Show*.

Following his one-year tenure at Eastland (he was fired), Dykes went on a barnstorming circuit, coaching at high schools in Ballinger, San Angelo, Coahoma, Belton, Big Spring, Alice, and Midland Lee.

To his credit, Spike Dykes is a down-to-earth guy who never claimed to be anyone other than himself. When once asked why he transferred from Rice to a junior college, Dykes joked: "Rice didn't offer the academic challenges I was seeking."

"Get to know the superintendent's secretary and the maintenance man first thing. You add the cafeteria lady, and you've got all the bases covered."

—— Dykes, on the first rule of high school coaching

"I DIDN'T CARE MUCH ABOUT COACHING THE DALLAS COWBOYS OR NOTRE DAME. MY GOAL WAS TO BE THE HEAD COACH AT BRADY OR MASON. AND I TRIED 10 MILLION YEARS TO GET THE SNYDER JOB. STARTING OUT THAT FIRST YEAR, I TRIED FOR THE ASSISTANT SEVENTH-GRADE JOB IN PORT NECHES. COULDN'T GET THAT. I TRIED FOR THE JUNIOR HIGH JOB IN TYLER. COULDN'T GET THAT."

—— Dykes

"I've been doing this awhile. I don't guess I've ever had a better win. Aspermont-Coleman in 1965 was the biggest. But I believe this one topped it."

—— Dykes, after a 38-8 upset win over Oklahoma, 1999

82

"MY WIFE CAME HOME AFTER WE LOST, AND SHE WAS SORT OF TEARED UP AND LOOKING LIKE SHE'D BEEN HIT IN THE FACE WITH A SKILLET. SHE SAID SHE WAS AT THE POST OFFICE AND THESE TWO RANCHERS SAID WE NEEDED TO FIRE THAT STUPID COACH BECAUSE IF HE WOULD HAVE PLAYED THE OTHER QUARTERBACK WE WOULD HAVE WON THAT BI-DISTRICT GAME. SO SOME THINGS NEVER CHANGE. I GUESS THAT WAS KIND OF THE TALK RADIO OF WEST TEXAS IN 1964."

—— Dykes, facing mounting criticism at Tech and recalling his first job at Coahoma High School, where he took over an 0-10 team and led it to an 11-1 record

"IT WAS PROBABLY A BAD PLAY CALL GOING FOR THE QUARTERBACK SNEAK. I THOUGHT IT MIGHT WORK, BUT IT DIDN'T. IF YOU'RE LOOKING FOR SOMEONE TO BLAME, BLAME ME. DON'T EVER BLAME A KID FOR TRYING TO WIN A GAME."

—— Dykes, after quarterback Zebbie Lethridge fumbled on a quarterback sneak as he neared the end zone on what would have been a go-ahead touchdown during a loss to Kansas State

"We've got a two-game season left. We need to win those two games or we'll be at grandma's house for Christmas."

—— Dykes, on needing two wins to earn a bowl bid, 1994

"My wife left for a three-week trip, and she recommended I drop a few pounds by the time she gets back. It's kind of like tossing one deck chair off the Queen Mary."

—— Dykes, on his diet, 1995

> **"We had to win our way here. We didn't buy three Big Macs and get a free ticket to the game."**
> —— Dykes, on his 6-5 team earning a Cotton Bowl berth, 1994

"Moby Dick was a minnow the last time we showed up here."
—— Dykes, referring to Tech's last Cotton Bowl appearance in 1939

"... IT'S KIND OF LIKE PLAYING IN THE U.S. OPEN FOR THE FIRST TIME. YOU BOGEY THE FIRST TWO OR THREE HOLES AND, DAD-GUM, IT'S HARD TO BREAK PAR. THAT'S WHAT HAPPENED TO US. IT WAS LIKE BOOM! BOOM! BOOM! WE BOGEYED THE FIRST THREE RIGHT OFF THE BAT."
—— Dykes, after Tech fell behind 28-0 to USC in the first quarter of the Cotton Bowl

"It looked like a spare or strike. It cut a swatch like a combine in a wheat field. He took them all out for about 10 yards square. I got two coaches who can hardly walk."
—— Dykes, after a 6-8, 360-pound Baylor defender crashed into the sideline, 1995

"I'm proud to be 4-0 this season. But we know we're not ready for Russia yet. We're not ready to say we're going to kill everybody and put a scalp on our belts."
—— Dykes, 1998

84

"WE HAD A ONE-NIGHT STAND. WE WERE EITHER GOING TO BE CONTENDERS OR PRETENDERS TODAY, SO I GUESS WE WERE PRETENDERS."

—— Dykes, on being ranked after his 22nd ranked team lost

"It's hard riding off into the sunset. I was born over there across the street, and my grandmother lived over there on Broadway. My mom and dad both went to Texas Tech. I don't know of anyone who is more proud of being a Red Raider than I am."

—— Dykes

"TOMMY'S THE HARDEST WORKING MAN I'VE EVER KNOWN. HE'S A CHRISTIAN MAN, A GOOD FAMILY MAN. BUT I USED TO READ HOW (PHILADELPHIA COACH) DICK VERMEIL WAS SUCH A HARD WORKER AND I'D LAUGH. THERE'S NO PLANO MYSTIQUE. IT'S HARD WORK AND COACHING. IT HAS TO BE THE MOST DISCIPLINED SPORTS PROGRAM ANYWHERE, PRO OR COLLEGE, BECAUSE THE KIDS ARE A CAPTIVE AUDIENCE. IT COULDN'T BE ANY MORE SOPHISTICATED OR ORGANIZED."

—— Plano High football team doctor Neal Small, on Wildcats' coach Tom Kimbrough, 1987

"It's probably the greatest cohesive force we have in schools. It's a chance for a lot of the old hands to relive their younger years."

—— Spring Westfield coach Emory Bellard, on Friday night football in Texas

"I've been asked for my least favorite memory. It wasn't dealing with coaches. They were sweethearts compared to cheerleaders' mothers."

—— Businessman Ross Perot, on his involvement in Texas education reform, 1995

"What are we going to do? Are we going to get in a fight over who starts at quarterback Friday night? Or the drum major for the band? We're going to have TEA deciding . . .? Give me a break. This is a farce."

—— Tyler ISD Superintendent Tom Hagler, after a Tyler drill team member appealed to the Texas Education Agency after not being named an officer, 1994

"MY GOAL IN LIFE IS TO BUILD A HOUSE FOR MY MOTHER SO THAT WHEN SHE LIES DOWN AT NIGHT SHE CAN'T SEE THE BIG DIPPER."

—— Tyler John Tyler running back Earl Campbell, 1974

"WE'RE EXPECTING A HUGE, STANDING-ROOM-ONLY CROWD AT THE GAME, AND ALTHOUGH WE'LL HAVE LAW ENFORCEMENT OUT IN FULL FORCE, IT'S ONLY PRUDENT THAT CHILDREN NOT BE ALLOWED ON THE STREET FRIDAY NIGHT."

—— Ganado mayor Dana Parks, on the decision to move Halloween up one night so not to conflict with the Ganado-Industrial football game between two unbeaten state-ranked teams, 1997

"I think religion is a private, personal thing. Keep it to yourself. Quit trying to change the world according to what you believe. And you know what? Football games — I don't think there's God anywhere within 50 yards of it. That's like a boxer getting in there and saying a prayer about going over to try to knock the other guy's brains out. And then when it's over, 'I want to thank my Lord.' "

—— Singer Waylon Jennings, when asked if there should be public prayers at football games in Texas, 2000

"It's brought everybody together 100 percent. Religion and football are the two things that keep Celina going."

—— Celina barbecue restaurant co-owner Rick Loftice, 2001

"LADIES AND GENTLEMEN, MARIAN WARD, A SANTA FE HIGH SCHOOL STUDENT, HAS BEEN SELECTED BY HER PEERS TO DELIVER A MESSAGE OF HER OWN CHOICE. THE SANTA FE INDEPENDENT SCHOOL DISTRICT DOES NOT REQUIRE, SUGGEST OR ENDORSE THE CONTENTS OF MS. WARD'S CHOICE OF A PRE-GAME MESSAGE."

—— Public address announcer, prior to pre-game prayer, 1999

"You still have a feel of Hometown USA here. It's like Mayberry RFD. My favorite time to live in this town is the day of our homecoming parade. The church is still a focal point of this town — the church or football."

—— Forney businesswoman Sandra Wilson, 2000

"I PLAYED FOOTBALL IN TEXAS, WHERE 15,000 PEOPLE WOULD SHOW UP FOR A HIGH SCHOOL FOOTBALL GAME. I ALWAYS SAID IF YOU WANT TO BURGLARIZE SOMEBODY'S HOUSE IN TEXAS, WAIT UNTIL FRIDAY NIGHT AT 8 P.M. AND THEN GO GET WHAT YOU WANT. IN TEXAS, IT'S SO VICIOUS THAT THEY WILL BOO A 15-YEAR-OLD KID, AND THESE ARE THE PARENTS. I WAS 17 YEARS OLD, A JUNIOR, AND I NEVER FORGOT THROWING THE BALL OUT OF BOUNDS AND LOOKING INTO THE STANDS AND THE PREACHER OF MY CHURCH IS BOOING ME LIKE I HAVE SINNED AGAINST JESUS."

—— Actor Jamie Foxx, on the set of the Oliver Stone movie, "Any Given Sunday," 1999

"It's hard to find people who are patriotic about things. The school song, when a lot of people are standing and singing...it's a very thrilling thing to me. A football game involves such a great percentage of the students. It's one thing that can actually pull your town together."

—— Former Brownwood coach Gordon Wood, 1991

"A FRIDAY NIGHT FOOTBALL GAME BRINGS THE COMMUNITY TOGETHER. IT'S AS MUCH OF A SOCIAL GATHERING AS IT IS INTEREST IN THE GAME ITSELF. IT'S NOT JUST ABOUT PLAYING THE GAME. IT'S ANOTHER PART OF THE EDUCATION SYSTEM. YOU CAN OVEREMPHASIZE ANYTHING, BUT I THINK WE KEEP OUR VALUES STRAIGHT."

—— Rockwall High coach Mark Elam, 2004

"This (state championship game) really does bring the whole town together. We've got gangs on the streets and they might shoot your (butt) tomorrow, but they'll love you at the game today."

—— Anonymous La Marque High School fan, during La Marque's 31-8 Class 4A state title win over Denison, 1995

"We are going to send over a school bus for Friday night's football game against Commerce. When you are in Bonham, Texas, that's one of the most exciting things that can happen to you on a Friday night."

—— Bonham ISD Superintendent Linda Gist, on inviting evacuees from Hurricane Katrina, who were staying in an armory in Bonham, to a football game, 2005

"THERE IS NO ACCOUNTABILITY IN THE PUBLIC SCHOOL SYSTEM – EXCEPT FOR COACHES. YOU KNOW WHAT HAPPENS TO A LOSING COACH. YOU FIRE HIM. A LOSING TEACHER CAN GO ON LOSING FOR THIRTY YEARS AND THEN GO TO GLORY."

—— Ross Perot, on Texas public education, 1984

"When you go to places that are tradition-rich, then you take a chance with your career because it's harder. There's more pressure to perform where people expect it. In Plano, Texas, they expect to win. In Waxahachie, Texas, they expect you to win. The only (job) security you have is winning."

— Plano East High coach Scott Phillips

"It's (Groveton) just a little Odessa Permian is all it is. You either win or you're gone. The school board didn't try to fire me; the parents did."

— Phillips, on coaching at Groveton High

"It's probably one of the highest pressure coaching jobs outside the Cowboys. But it's also one of the best places to be."

— Hebron High School defensive coordinator Dane Johnson, on the vacant Southlake Carroll High job, 2006

"It's like being home, not on foreign soil anymore. I knew I didn't want to go back to colleges. I never felt at home at North Texas, or in the (Denton) community."

— New Cleburne High coach Dennis Parker, who had been fired previously at the University of North Texas, 1994

"There's two ways to hire a coach. There can be one person who's in charge, and they are making the decision. Then there's the way to do it so nobody has to take the blame if something goes wrong. Then they do it by committee."

— Cleburne High School football coach/athletic director Dennis Parker, 1997

"I was re-hired as a teacher and told I wouldn't be the football coach. That was pretty plain. People at the American Legion, if they lose money (betting on games), they get hostile."

— Former Tidehaven coach Don Godwin, 1994

"High school kids always emulate the pros and college and always will. Coaches don't have the control, respect and discipline they used to. I couldn't coach now. They'd fire me."

— Kedric Couch, who coached football in Dallas high schools from 1954-88, 1996

"Half my kids don't have a lot of role models. Coaching's not like it was 36 years ago. You went and coached and went home. Now you coach, and you father and you counsel."

— Dallas Molina coach Charles DeVille, 2005

"TO ME, COACHING HAS NEVER BEEN A JOB. I LOVE IT AND WOULD DO IT FOR NOTHING ... I'VE BEEN LUCKY IN MY LIFE — COACHING HAS NEVER BEEN LIKE WORK."

— Celina coach G. A. Moore, 1995

90

"Frank Bevers is the reason I coach today. He changed my life. It was more than just a game. The game was a small part of it. The part he also taught was about being a good guy – the part about when you're in the school building helping somebody out. He coached us hard. He was rough. He was a country bumpkin come to the city. But Coach loved us. He cared about you in all areas of your life."

—— Odessa Permian coach Scott Smith, on the former Highland Park coach

"I haven't met a coach yet that didn't think he was Moses and could lead anyone out of the wilderness. It's that kind of arrogance that usually makes them good."

—— Irving ISD athletic director Don Poe, 1995

"If you look at my history, I don't move around a lot. I mean in 16 years I've been in just two towns. Not many preachers can say that. I've been fortunate."

—— Sherman High coach John Outlaw, on taking the Lufkin job, 1995

"HE IS ONE OF THE SMALL HANDFUL OF COACHES WHO IS GOING TO WIN WHEREVER HE GOES. HE CAN GET WATER OUT OF A ROCK."

—— North Mesquite coach Steve Bragg, on new Carrollton Creekview coach Gary Childress, who was returning to the sidelines after a 15-year career as an athletic director, 2005

"When I came here, I thought this would be our permanent home, but I guess there's no such thing as permanent in high school coaching."

—— Carrollton R. L. Turner High coach Bootsie Larsen, resigning with a 1-27-2 record

"We'd have to see Jesus coming out on the 50-yard line. I mean it would take that kind of miracle. Or maybe if coach (Bob) Brown brought one of those 12-year-old youth football teams out here."

—— Wichita Falls Hirschi High coach Tom Chancellor, when asked what it would take for his 1-7-1 team to upset Denison in 1995 (Denison won, 64-0, en route to a 15-1 season).

"I'LL PLAY THE DALLAS COWBOYS IF THEY'LL SCHEDULE ME. CARTER HIGH SCHOOL WILL PLAY ANYBODY. WE WANT TO BE THE BEST WE CAN BE, SO WE WANT TO PLAY THE BEST."

—— Dallas Carter coach Bruce Chambers, on his tough scheduling, 1997

"I don't care if we're playing the Dallas Cowboys. They (Marshall) probably could play with the Cowboys. They're scary. I can see why they're ranked so high. Try to find a non-athlete on that team. You can't."

—— Dallas Bryan Adams High coach Randy Walker, after his school qualified for the playoffs for the first time in 11 years and was to play second-ranked Marshall, 1996

"Lake Highlands is a great team. They run the wishbone as well as Oklahoma used to run it."

—— Jersey Village coach Rudy Phillips, after a 17-13 playoff loss to Lake Highlands, 1995

"IT DOESN'T REALLY MATTER TO ME WHO WE PLAY. IF WE HAD TO PLAY OKLAHOMA THE FIRST GAME, WE WOULD PUT ON OUR HELMET AND PLAY THEM BECAUSE MY KIDS AND I ARE SO EXCITED TO BE IN THE PLAYOFFS."

—— Dallas W.T. White High coach Mike Zoffuto, 2000

"They've got more athletes than Texas A&M."

—— Bryan Adams High coach Randy Walker, on Dallas Carter, 1995

"I always had a tremendous desire to play. I just enjoyed it. You were in high school and you got a letter jacket and that meant you would have a girlfriend. And then you found out you got silver football patches for making all-district and you could put them on your jacket and they look good. The town would throw a banquet if you won district. There weren't a lot of people in town, but they were all involved with the team. I loved it."

—— Former Dallas Cowboys and Hall-of-Famer Bob Lilly

"I wanted to be a football player. I think we (Texans) were all expected to play football. It was an endeavor that was respected by adults and kids alike. It provided something that a young man could do for himself to create responsibility and achievement. I think most of the young men in Texas were hungry for that."

—— Actor Tommy Lee Jones, on growing up in Texas

"In high school I was only 140 pounds. And in Texas, when you're too small for football, they send you to drama class."

— Actor Dennis Quaid

"WE SCREWED UP THE KICKING GAME BIG TIME. FOR FIVE WEEKS IN A ROW, WE'VE BEEN PERFECT. I DON'T KNOW WHAT HAPPENED TONIGHT. I GUESS THAT'S WHAT GIVES OLD COACHES GRAY HAIR."

— McKinney High coach Ron Poe, after a 24-6 loss to district rival Highland Park, 1997

"If I was presented with the situation and I needed a kicker, I probably would. I'd use my dog if I had to."

— Denison High coach Bob Brown, when asked if he'd consider using a female place-kicker, 2005

"Two-thousand kids at that school and you'd think they could get one who can take a (expletive) kickoff."

— Middle-aged woman talking to her husband in the stands at Ratliff Stadium after an Odessa Permian player mishandled a kickoff, 1994

"WE TELL THE PLAYERS A COUPLE OF WEEKS BEFORE THAT WE COULD BE PLAYING ON THANKSGIVING, SO DON'T BE MAKING PLANS TO GO TO GRANDMA'S IN KANSAS."

— Grapevine High coach Mike Sneed, 1999

"He was Superman playing among boys. I was the last guy to block anything in the hole before he came through. If I didn't get my block, he'd come through anyway. Even if it meant going over me."

— Former Sugar Land wingback Jerry Cooper, a teammate of legendary running back Kenneth Hall

"I ALWAYS THOUGHT SUPERMAN WAS WHITE, BUT HE'S NOT. HE'S BLACK, WEARS NUMBER 20, AND PLAYS FOR JOHN TYLER."

—— Conroe High coach W.T. Stapler, on the exploits of Tyler running back Earl Campbell

"I never thought I'd be able to say, if we just could have held their running back to 275 yards, we would have won the game."

—— Hurst L.D. Bell High coach Jack Gibson, after Irving High's Tyson Thompson rushed for 526 yards in a 45-29 victory, 1998

"IT SOUNDS LIKE TEXAS HIGH SCHOOL FOOTBALL HAS GONE SOFT."

—— Buzz Bissinger, author of "Friday Night Lights," when told that sushi would be served in the concession stand at Southlake Carroll games, 2008

"Everybody should have a chance to play Odessa Permian at least once, and that's probably enough."

—— Fort Worth Trimble Tech High coach Quintin Robinson

"Oil is still Number 1 out here, next to God and high school football. It affects everything out here. When the oilfield's doing well and Mojo's doing good, that (printed game program) gets real big."

—— Odessa Permian booster club president Tony Cunningham, 1998

"The rest of the world is sweeping past us. The oil and gas of the Texas future is the well-educated mind. But we are still worried about whether Midland can beat Odessa at football."

—— Mark White, Governor of Texas

"GENTLEMEN, THE HOPES AND DREAMS OF AN ENTIRE TOWN ARE RIDING ON YOUR SHOULDERS. YOU MAY NEVER MATTER AGAIN IN YOUR LIFE AS MUCH AS YOU DO RIGHT NOW."

—— Billy Bob Thornton, portraying Odessa Permian coach Gary Gaines in the movie "Friday Night Lights"

"Our kids believe they have a chance to beat Celina. I'll tell you this, it's no secret about who we are. We're a bunch of ranchers and kids working in the oil fields out there. We're not as talented as Celina, everybody knows that, but we have a lot of heart."

—— Sonora High coach Jason Herring, as his 12-2 team prepared to play 14-0 Celina in a Class 2A state semifinal game. Celina won, 35-13, en route to the state title, 2001

"God bless those kids. I'm sick. I want to throw up."

—— Lake Highlands coach Mike Zofutto, broadcasting a playoff game in which Plano East was beaten in the final seconds by Tyler John Tyler on a 97-yard kickoff return, 1994

"People outside this community have some wrong ideas about this community. They think we have spoiled rich kids who won't work hard. But that's not the case...These kids are simply doing what they see their parents do. Their families are success-oriented. They see their parents working hard. They prepare for success because that's what they've seen."

—— Highland Park High coach Frank Bevers

"WEALTH HAS NOTHING TO DO WITH WINNING. HIGHLAND PARK DOESN'T WIN BECAUSE THEY'RE WEALTHY. THEY WIN BECAUSE THEY'RE DISCIPLINED."

—— Plano East High coach Scott Phillips

"Football is like anything else, it follows technology. In 1965, we were using calculators. Now we use computers."

—— Arlington High School coach Bill Keith, 1996

"YOU DON'T WIN WITH THE BEST ATHLETES. YOU WIN WHEN YOUR KIDS BELIEVE IN EACH OTHER AND FEEL LIKE THEY ARE GOING TO WIN. THAT'S WHY WE HAD OUR PLAYERS TALKING TO JUNIOR HIGH AND ELEMENTARY KIDS ABOUT BEING A CARROLL DRAGON. THOSE KIDS GROW UP WANTING TO BE NO. 1."

—— Former Southlake Carroll High coach Bob Ledbetter, on the importance of tradition

"TOO MUCH ADULATION AND GLORY IS NOT A GOOD THING...ARE THESE KIDS GOING TO LIVE THEIR LIVES IN QUIET DESPERATION ONCE THE CHEERS GO AWAY? HIGH SCHOOL FOOTBALL IN AND OF ITSELF IS ENOUGH. WE DON'T NEED THE TELEVISION LIGHTS."

—— Author "Buzz" Bissinger, on the telecasting of high school football games, 2004

"He's got more character than any kid I've ever coached. If I had 11 like him, all I would need is a bus driver."

—— Dallas Bryan Adams High coach Mike Smiddy, on Hurricane Katrina evacuee and move-in Christian Riley, a quarterback from Buras High School in Louisiana, 2005

"The algebra teacher used to coach football. Now the football coach teaches algebra."

—— Hall of Fame football player Sammy Baugh, on why high school football improved over the years in Texas

"The game of football has as much to teach a kid as sitting in an English or algebra class."

—— Kilgore High coach Mike Vallery

"Teachers complained they never got enough recognition for what happened in this community. You go out and take your English class and put it in front of 12,000 people in Wildcat Stadium, and maybe people will recognize what you do. See, my work was on the line every Friday night. People aren't going to pay five bucks a head to watch them teach an English class."

—— Former Lake Highlands High coach Mike Zoffuto

"THE GOOD THING ABOUT OUR SCHEDULE IS THAT WE DON'T HAVE TO TRAVEL VERY FAR. THERE'S NO REASON TO GO A LONG WAYS TO GET YOUR BUTT BEAT WHEN YOU CAN DO IT CLOSER TO HOME."

—— Keller Fossil Ridge High coach Richard Dibble, 1998

"We kissed our sister. I don't like kissing my sister, but at least I've got a pretty sister. By pretty sister, I mean a team that can play. And Carter definitely can play."

—— Dallas Kimball High coach James Jones, on his team's 0-0 tie with rival Dallas Carter, 1994

"This game is oddly important to people around here. You know as well as I do what it means to the people around here. I kind of got my tail chewed out my first year because I didn't place as great a value on this game as I should have."

—— Denison High coach Bob Brown, after beating arch-rival Sherman for the first time, 1995

"The knuckleheads and goofballs that were doing stupid stuff are all in their 40s and 50s now."

—— Dallas Jesuit High coach Bob Wunderlick, on resuming his school's rivalry with Bishop Lynch after a 16-year hiatus due to fights and vandalism, 2006

"HE'S GOT TO BE THE HIGHEST-SCORING TACKLE IN TEXAS."

—— Azle High coach Buddy Brock, on Azle tackle Lyle Brister, who returned three fumble recoveries for touchdowns during the season, 1995

"We have been hurt all year. We knew if we could just get people back, we could play. Half our defense has been out. We've had people out the last three games, but even the dead come back to play this game."

—— Dallas Kimball High coach James Jones, after a 21-7 win over arch-rival Dallas Carter

"People I don't even know have been coming up to me and saying, 'Great game last week,' and my mom cries before and after every game."

—— Farmersville High wide receiver Jared Helmberger, on the community's excitement during a playoff run in which the Farmers won their first-ever state football title, 2007

99

"OFFENSIVELY, THIS WAS OUR BEST GAME OF THE YEAR. THE OFFENSIVE LINE EXECUTED, WE MOVED THE BALL, BUT JUST CAME UP SHORT."

—— Bonham High coach John Hall, after a 25-0 loss to Van Alstyne, 2008

✳ **10** ✳

MOST POLITICALLY INCORRECT
TEXAS SPORTS QUOTES

1. *"I am really happy to be back in Calgary, I love Canada. I just want to comment on how it's become like a common thing in the NHL for guys to fall in love with my sloppy seconds. I don't know what that's about. Enjoy the game tonight."*— Dallas Stars forward Sean Avery, at a press conference, talking about an NHL player who was dating his ex-girlfriend. Avery was suspended indefinitely by the league for detrimental conduct. 2008

2. *"N.O.W. (National Organization for Women) is such a blowhard organization. They are a bunch of lesbians."* — Houston Astros pitcher Bob Knepper, 1988

3. *"This is not an occupation a woman should be in. In God's society, woman was created in a role of submission to the husband. It's not that woman is inferior, but I don't believe woman should be in a leadership role."* — Knepper, on a woman trying to be a major league umpire, 1988

4. *"I don't understand where that came from. For that to be out there, I don't want fans thinking it was something as silly as a woman."* — Jason Kidd of the Dallas Mavericks, on the rumor that a woman was the cause of a feud between him and teammate Jim Jackson, 1996

5. *"I know we don't have any Dallas people here. They're the ugliest people in the world."* — Washington Redskins coach Joe Gibbs, during Fan Appreciation Day at Redskins Park, 2005

6. *"They're the pick of the litter."* — Jerry Jones, on the Dallas Cowboys cheerleaders

7. *"You may be proud of Lubbock today, but I'm sick of it. We need some good things from another recruiting year, but we won't get them unless you fans wise up."* — Texas Tech football coach Jim Carlen, to a booster club, 1971

8. *"John ran like a tush hog. He ran around like a greased pig. He*

101

really ran hard tonight. He came to win." — Plano East coach Scott Phillips, on running back John Leake's 156-yard rushing effort in a win over rival Plano High, 1999

9. *"You don't see many minority athletes in our program. It's very obvious to me the other day that the other team had a lot more Afro-American players than we did. It just seems to be the way that Afro-American kids can run very, very well. That doesn't mean that Caucasian kids and other descents can't run, but it's very obvious to me they run extremely well."* — Air Force football coach Fisher DeBerry, who was reprimanded by school officials for these comments after a 48-10 loss to TCU, 2005

10. *"What…and leave college coaching to the (Barry) Switzers and (Jackie) Sherrills?"* — Penn State coach Joe Paterno, when asked if he would ever give up coaching to enter politics, 1979

"5"

"Send in the Clowns"

A E "Abe" Lemons was arguably the funniest, most quotable, and most sought-after banquet speaking coach in the history of intercollegiate athletics. He was also a brilliant college basketball coach, winning 599 games during a 34-year career that included stops at Oklahoma City University, Pan American University, and the University of Texas.

Lemons favored a high-scoring offensive attack, but his on-court success was often overshadowed by his opinionated quotes off-the-court. Unlike most coaches, Lemons spoke with refreshing candor and honesty. He also had the rare knack of making a serious point with a humorous, if often sarcastic, remark.

No less an expert than legendary basketball coach Bob Knight once wrote of Lemons:

"Abe has one of the five best basketball minds I have encountered during my time in coaching. Just like his fellow Oklahoman, Will Rogers, Abe's wisdom comes through very clearly to those who just listen to him carefully while he talks. He is the most entertaining person I have ever seen in athletics."

Lemons' biting wit entertained media and fans, spared no one, and frequently caught the ire of referees, opponents, and even university administrators. His own players were many times subjected to his straight-shooting remarks, but they seemed to respond with positive results. It seemed that officiating crews, communists, and Arkansas all had about the same "value" to "Honest Abe."

While hugely successful at Texas from 1976-82, the popular Lemons was fired from the school. No specifics for the controversial firing were offered by athletic director DeLoss Dodds. However, the unspoken reason for the dismissal was the fact that many of Lemons' non-politically-correct musings did not represent the "corporate" image of a state institution such as the University of Texas.

Back in his heyday at UT, Lemons' offbeat sense of humor was aptly demonstrated during the 1978 season.

In the late stages of the Southwest Conference race that year, Lemons told reporters that his team was "dead" because it trailed Arkansas in the standings. But after Arkansas was upset by Houston and Texas moved into a tie for first, Lemons opened his Sunday night television show as follows:

The camera zoomed in on a prone Lemons clad in a dark suit with a carnation in his folded hands. Soft music played in the background. The "corpse" rose slowly, turned to the camera, and shouted, "We're not dead yet!"

Sure enough, his Longhorns went on to earn a co-championship with the Razorbacks. UT lost to Houston in the championship game of the SWC post-season tournament and did not receive a bid to the NCAA tourney. However, the Longhorns were invited to the National Invitational Tournament and advanced to the finals at Madison Square Garden in New York City, where they defeated North Carolina State.

Earlier that season, during a routine 78-64 whipping of Rice in Austin, Owls coach Mike Schuler felt compelled to make 99 substitutions against Texas. Afterwards, Lemons noted, "all they needed were clowns to make it a circus."

A few weeks later, when the teams met at Autry Court in Houston, hundreds of Rice students dressed up for "Clown Night." It made little difference, as Texas cruised to a 102-86 victory. And Abe had this to say about the proceedings:

"I like the circus, always have. As far as the clowns go, I've faced the Japanese and Germans in World War II. I've walked the snowdrifts of Buffalo and the wharves in Calcutta at 2 a.m. I've seen wharf rats bigger than some of those clowns. No clown is going to bother me."

"You can say something to popes, kings, and presidents. But you can't talk to officials. In the next war, they ought to give everybody a whistle."

— Lemons

"SOME ALUMNI OFFERED TO BUY OUT MY CONTRACT. I TOLD THEM I DIDN'T HAVE CHANGE FOR A TWENTY."

— Lemons

"Doctors bury their mistakes. We still have ours on scholarship."

— Lemons

"I TOLERATE DEFENSE, BUT I LIKE OFFENSE. IN EVERY GAME WE'VE EVER WON, WE ALWAYS OUTSCORED THE OTHER GUY."

— Lemons

"THERE ARE ONLY TWO PLAYS: 'ROMEO AND JULIET' AND PUT THE DARN BALL IN THE BASKET."

— Lemons, on strategy

107

"We went to Alaska once and they made us honorary Alaskans. Then we went to Hawaii and they made us honorary Hawaiians. Then we went to the Virgin Islands."

— Lemons, on his exotic road trips

"If you win and say that such and such a player is slow, everyone laughs. It's funny when you win. If you lose, and you say the same thing, all of a sudden it's criticism. The truth, I guess, is a whole lot funnier when you're winning."

— Lemons, on criticizing players

"I'm not saying coaches shouldn't be fired. I just think you should be faced by your accusers. Hell, when (John) Hinckley shot the President (Reagan), they gave him a trial."

— Lemons, on not being allowed to face his accusers

"I WANT TO BE IN A GLASS-BOTTOM CAR SO I CAN SEE HIS FACE WHEN I RUN OVER HIM."

— Lemons, after he was fired by athletic director DeLoss Dodds

"I hope they notice the mistletoe tied to my coattails as I leave town."

— Lemons, on his firing

"I got fired from the University of Texas. I didn't deserve that. Now I've got Parkinson's disease. I don't deserve that, either."

— Lemons, 1990

"People ask me if I'm still bitter. You're damn right I am. I knew you'd like hearing that. You get fired by a track coach (DeLoss Dodds). That's about the most degrading thing that can happen to you. It's like getting fired by a volleyball coach."
— Lemons, when asked in 1993 about being fired by Texas

"THE PROGRAM WILL CENTER AROUND GOOD PEOPLE, GOOD ATHLETES AND GOOD WORKERS. THEY'LL BE STUDENTS FIRST, PLAYERS SECOND. WE'RE GOING TO DO IT WITH CHARACTER, NOT CHARACTERS."

— Newly-hired University of Texas coach Bob Weltlich, 1982

"It's just amazing that one single event would have had such a profound effect on so many lives and careers. It was a happening. We now have three pro basketball teams in Texas. You would never have thought we would have these facilities for basketball in Texas, because Texas was a football state."
— Former pro basketball player Elvin Hayes, recalling the 1968 Houston-UCLA basketball game, played in the Astrodome. Hayes starred for the Houston Cougars.

"I DON'T THINK I'VE PLAYED FOR ANY BETTER COACH. COACH (GUY) LEWIS GAVE ME A VERY STRONG FOUNDATION IN THIS COUNTRY. THE WORK ETHIC. THE MENTAL TOUGHNESS TO DO WHAT IT TAKES IN COLLEGE. HE EXPECTED YOU TO GIVE YOUR BEST ALWAYS. IT WAS A VERY GOOD START FOR ME."
— Houston Rockets center Hakeem Olajuwon, on his college coach, Houston's Guy Lewis

"IF YOU WANT TO HAVE A CIRCUS, PUT A TENT OVER IT."

— University of Texas coach Tom Penders, expressing his displeasure with the officiating at the SWC Tournament in 1990

"The basket was disallowed because of offensive pass interference."

— Texas A&M public address announcer, on a goaltending call during an Aggie-Houston game

"I hate the (A&M) fight song, and I hate the wave they do. We even have Aggies in our state. They used to be Oklahoma A&M, but they upgraded to Oklahoma State."

— University of Oklahoma coach Billy Tubbs, 1990

"It was anybody's game, and we came up short. As Bobby Layne would say, we didn't lose, we just ran out of time."

— Texas coach Tom Penders, after a 75-73 loss to Texas Tech in the SWC post-season tournament championship game, 1996

"I don't believe we have to do that (be successful) by cheating. The patient is sick and needs a few shots in the arm. But I believe we can bring it back to where it can compete. There will not be a quick fix. I will not be part of that."

— New Baylor coach Harry Miller, taking over a scandal-filled program, 1995

"TEXAS TECH IS A GREAT BALL CLUB, AND IF THEY'RE NOT ONE OF THE TOP 30 TEAMS IN THE NATION, I'M GOING TO SELL SHOES. SOME OF MY ALUMNI THINK I SHOULD ALREADY."
— Texas coach Tom Penders, 1995

"I feel like a crime's been committed. Somebody on that (selection) committee needs to be arrested. I feel like the child who runs out on Christmas morning and there's nothing under the tree … We got screwed. But let's lace up the shoes and play."
— Texas guard Roderick Anderson, on the Longhorns' being seeded 11th for the NCAA Tournament, 1995

"No kid ever comes to a school saying, 'I really want to be a good defensive player.' "
— Texas A&M coach Tony Barone

"LAST YEAR WE WERE THE WORST DEFENSIVE TEAM GUARDING THE DRIBBLE I'VE EVER SEEN. WE COULDN'T HAVE GUARDED MICKEY MOUSE IF HE WAS DRIBBLING THE BASKETBALL."
— Barone, 1995

"The Baylor Bears have just embarrassed Tommy Penders and the 23rd-ranked Texas Longhorns, 76-72."
— Baylor public address announcer Brad Cox, chiding the Longhorns immediately after the upset, 1997

"I've never considered the Texas-Baylor thing a real rivalry, but it will be. What was said will be put up on everybody's locker before that game for as long as I'm the coach here."
— Texas coach Tom Penders, 1997

"I guess it's hard to overcome Madison Square Garden, the Catholics and ESPN."

—— TCU athletic director Frank Windegger, after the decision was made that TCU, with a record of 22-12, would have to travel to Notre Dame (15-13) to play a second round NIT game, 1997

"I am one of the luckiest guys in the world. I rebuilt a sorry program into one of the best in the country, got $1 million to leave and ended up with a better job. I am not bitter. I only have bitterness towards one guy, the shill who is the athletic director (DeLoss Dodds). The athletic director undermined my program. I wanted out of there. There is not an athletic director in the country who could get away with it unless he had pictures of somebody at a Christmas party."

—— George Washington University coach Tom Penders, reflecting on his tenure at the University of Texas, 1999

"HE RUNS THE FLOOR EXTREMELY WELL AND HE FLAT OUTRAN US TONIGHT. HIS STRENGTH IS ALSO A BIG FACTOR. WE LOOKED LIKE OLIVE OYL AND HE LOOKED LIKE BRUTUS. YOU KNOW WHO IS GOING TO WIN THAT MATCH-UP."

—— Baylor coach Harry Miller, on Texas Tech player Darvin Ham, after a 78-72 loss to Tech

"This (Texas) is a great job and I think DeLoss (Dodds) would be a great guy to work for. But I'm real happy. I like my AD. I like my players. I like Utah. It's like being a married guy, but Cindy Crawford comes over and asks you if you want to dance. It's kind of enticing to grab on for a dance. Then after the dance is over, you go back to your wife."

—— Utah coach Rick Majerus, when asked if he was interested in the Texas job, 1998

"It was a rat killing. They were doing the killing. You can guess who the rat was."

—— Miller, after his team lost to Texas 86-65 in the SWC Tournament, 1996

"To quote a coach who previously was here, we ain't dead yet."

—— Texas women's coach Jody Conradt, whose struggling team beat SMU, 1995

"I told our kids before the game that if our previous television performances had been a sitcom, we would have been cancelled. Thank goodness we performed better today."

—— Texas A&M women's coach Candi Harvey, after her team upset Texas in the SWC post-season tournament, 1996

"Her stamina is better than any player I've ever been around. She must have big lungs. But what makes it really amazing is that she's our leading scorer and our best perimeter defender, and she's still able to maintain her play."

—— University of Texas at Arlington women's coach Mike Dean, on player Natasha Johnson, 1997

"IT WAS VINTAGE AMIE SMITH. SHE SCRATCHED, CLAWED, AND BIT EVERYONE OUT THERE. THERE WERE TIMES SHE JUST WILLED THINGS OUR WAY."

—— Texas women's coach Jody Conradt, on Amie Smith, who scored 18 points, had 13 rebounds, eight steals and four assists in a win over Nebraska, 1997

"We have a young team, and they walked on the floor and saw that crowd. I think they got gawked out."

—— Baylor women's coach Sonja Hogg, after her team lost to Texas Tech, 74-59, before a crowd of 7,900 in Lubbock, 1996

"Billy Tubbs said beating Tulsa got the monkey off his back. You can say we got King Kong off our back."

—— TCU women's coach Jeff Mittie, after snapping a 19-game losing streak to SMU, 2001

"I'M NOT BATMAN. I CAN'T FLY OFF THE COURT THAT QUICKLY TO GET TO THE SIDELINE."

—— Texas A&M basketball coach Gary Blair, after being whistled for technical fouls and being ejected after walking onto the court to protest a call in an 84-59 loss to Baylor, 2006

"YOU DON'T HAVE A LOT OF MCDONALD'S ALL-AMERICANS. YOU HAVE KIDS WHO EAT AT BURGER KING WHO KNOW HOW TO PLAY BALL."

—— Blair, on Big 12 leader Nebraska, 2010

"You saw it. There's no place for that in sports. I will deal with Brittney Griner and it won't be discussed in the media. Not me or Kristy (Curry) or any player will be proud of what took place on the floor tonight."

— Baylor women's basketball coach Kim Mulkey, after Baylor's 6-8 center Brittney Griner floored a Texas Tech player with a punch during a game in Lubbock, 2010 (Griner was suspended for two games.)

"You're watching a phenom out here play above the rim. That's what needs to be written in every article from this day forward, because she's such a sweet child, as you can see."

— Mulkey, after Griner scored 27 rebounds and 10 blocked shots in a victory over Tennessee in the NCAA playoffs, 2010

"One night, he played two quarters in the B-team game and two in the varsity game, and he was the leading scorer in both games. He played strictly varsity after that."

— Clay (Ind.) High School athletic director Greg Humnicky, on TCU's Lee Nailon in high school, 1999

"HOW WOULD YOU LIKE TO HAVE TO WATCH THEM PLAY EVERY NIGHT? BEFORE YOU WATCH THEM, MAKE SURE YOU DON'T TAKE ANY MEDICATION. DON'T DRIVE OR USE HEAVY EQUIPMENT AFTER YOU PLAY THOSE GUYS BECAUSE YOU MIGHT FALL ASLEEP."

— TCU coach Billy Tubbs, after a 65-58 win over slow-paced San Jose State, 2001

"All the great players have ugly feet. That's where he's improved, his toenails are falling off. That means he's pushing off."

— University of Texas coach Rick Barnes, on his 7-foot center Chris Mihm

"I think the most realistic expectation we have is that we show up everywhere we're supposed to play."
—— New Texas Tech coach Bob Knight, 2001

"BASKETBALL, TO ME, HAS ALWAYS BEEN A GAME WHERE WHEN GUYS ARE PLAYING WELL, THEY PLAY, AND WHEN THEY DON'T, THEY DON'T. IT'S KIND OF A SIMPLE EQUATION, LIKE ONE PLUS ONE."

—— Knight, when asked why one of his starters played sparingly in the second half in a loss to TCU

"What they did to us was beautiful; unfortunately, I was coaching the other team. That was poetry out there, the way they were playing."

—— Texas A&M coach Billy Gillespie, after a 70-56 loss to Texas Tech

"I appreciate Billy saying that. But we're not reading the same poets."
—— Bob Knight, responding to Gillespie's praise

"I've seen a lot of things. Been to goat ropings, rodeos and cookoffs, but I don't know that I've ever been involved in a game like that."

—— Texas women's coach Jody Conradt, after her team rallied from a 14-point deficit in the second half to beat Oklahoma in overtime, 83-71, 2005

"We couldn't overpower Our Lady of the Harbor. But it was a very good win for us."
—— Bob Knight, after a 72-66 win over Baylor

116

"I don't want to bust my (expletive) all the time and have it turned over to somebody who has no idea what the hell they're doing or knows what coaching at Tech is all about. This way, it has somebody coming into it that is conducive to Tech and can maintain and improve things."

—— Knight, on the fact that when he retired, his son Pat would replace him, 2005 (Pat took over in mid-season 2007-08.)

"You guys invent too many things. You guys sometimes remind me of Thomas Edison."

-- Bob Knight, when asked by reporters if he thought upcoming opponent Colorado might have extra motivation because of their lame-duck coach Ricardo Patton, 2007

"I really appreciate the improvement that you are."

—— Tech coach Bob Knight, to new University Chancellor Kent Hance, at a post-game event celebrating Knight's breaking the record for most-ever NCAA career victories. A few years earlier, Knight had a highly publicized confrontation with then-chancellor David Smith at a Lubbock salad bar. 2007

"WINNING DOES MIRACULOUS THINGS FOR COACHING. IT'S AN ELIXIR BEYOND BELIEF. NOW, I WANT YOU TO FIND OUT IF YOU CAN EVER SEE IF A COACH EVER BEFORE WAS QUOTED USING THE WORD 'ELIXIR.' "

—— Bob Knight, in comments to the media

"There's a lot of guys in the NBA who can bench 300 pounds who couldn't play dead in a cowboy movie. Kevin's the best player in the draft, period."

—— Texas coach Rick Barnes, on questions about Kevin Durant's strength, 2007

"Have you guys ever seen the movie, 'The Terminator?' That's what that kid is like. That kid has no facial expressions. He just plays and it's like every kid out there on him is like Sarah Connor, and he's just going to take his time and kill him. That kid is good."

— Texas Tech coach Pat Knight, after a loss to Oklahoma and its star Blake Griffin

"I HAVE TO SAY, THESE GUYS HAVE GOT TWO THINGS — THEY'VE GOT HEART AND THEY'VE GOT CAJONES. I THINK I CAN SAY THAT WITHOUT GETTING INTO TROUBLE. THAT'S WHAT THIS TEAM HAS. I DON'T CARE WHAT THE RECORD IS, THIS TEAM HAS THOSE TWO THINGS. I'M PROUD OF THEM. I CAN'T SAY ANYTHING MORE THAN THAT. TO COME BACK LIKE THAT, AGAINST A GOOD TEAM LIKE THAT, JUST SAYS EVERYTHING ABOUT THESE GUYS."

— Tech coach Pat Knight, after his team rallied from a 21-point deficit to upset Texas A&M in the Big 12 Tournament, 2009

"I'd let my wife support me. I'd sit on the couch in a torn T-shirt, drink beer and watch Bob Newhart on TV."

— Dallas Mavericks forward Kurt Nimphius, when asked what he'd be doing if he weren't playing pro basketball, 1984

"LOOK, EVERYTHING I EVER DID IN DALLAS, EVERY PROBLEM THAT DICK MOTTA AND I EVER HAD, WAS BLOWN OUT OF PROPORTION. THE ONLY THING THAT WAS INTERESTING ABOUT THE DALLAS MAVERICKS WAS MY PROBLEMS."

— Mavericks forward Mark Aguirre, after being traded from Dallas to Detroit, 1989

"MARK COULD DOMINATE A GAME WHEN HE WANTED TO, ONLY WHEN HE WAS IN THE RIGHT FRAME OF MIND. YOU JUST CAN'T LET YOUR TEAMMATES DOWN, AND HE LET US DOWN A LOT."

—— Mavericks guard Rolando Blackman, on Aguirre

"We were our own worst enemy. It was like we were running uphill on flypaper all night. We were stumbling all over the floor. We fell down four times in the first half on the way to lay-ups."

—— Mavericks coach Dick Motta, after an 89-80 loss to Denver, 1994

"He doesn't have to say a word about what he's been through. It's like that commercial, when E.F. Hutton talks, people listen. He's E.F. Hutton."

—— Mavericks rookie Jason Kidd, on Motta

"I don't have any jerks. So I don't have to be a jerk in return. This is the way it was in high school, college, and with the Chicago Bulls. I never raised my voice."

—— Motta, on his 1994-95 team

"HE'S (ROY TARPLEY) NOT UNDER A MICROSCOPE. IT'S A TELESCOPE. BIGGER THAN THE HUBBLE."

—— Motta, on Tarpley and his aftercare program, 1995

"Every little thing I do just gets magnified. It just makes me really understand I'm in a glass house. I'm just going to stay in my glass house and tint the windows now."

—— Tarpley, after he received a speeding ticket at 3 a.m. and a friend wrecked his car an hour later, 1995

"First of all, I don't lend my car to people. My father always told me when I was young. 'Don't borrow anyone's rifle, car or try to get their wife.' I've tried to stick pretty much with that."

— Motta, on Tarpley's situation

"I HAVE NOTHING AGAINST THE ORGANIZATION. I THINK MOTTA IS A GOOD MAN AND ONE OF THE BEST COACHES IN THIS LEAGUE. I'LL GO TO MY GRAVE SAYING THAT."

— Tarpley

"You could write 1,000 books about him. I think he could have been one of the five best players who ever played the game. But he kept putting candy up his nose. I'll never understand. He was intelligent. A nice kid."

— Motta, recalling Tarpley's substance-abuse-plagued career, 2000

"Winners laugh and have a good time. Losers meet."

— Motta, on team meetings during a losing streak

"THEY CAN DO ONE OF TWO THINGS: GET IN THE FETAL POSITION AND GO BACK TO MAMA, OR THEY CAN COME BACK AND BE A PRO."

— Motta, on his team's slump

"We don't have a leader on this team. I was thinking about getting a sheep dog. I'd call it Sam. Old Sam."

— Motta

120

"I ONLY TRY TO JUDGE THINGS I SEE ON THE FLOOR. I GOT PAST BEING A SOCIAL DIRECTOR YEARS AND YEARS AGO."

—— Motta, when asked about two of his players who were feuding

"I think Hakeem (Olajuwon) is the best player on the planet."

—— Houston Rockets guard Clyde Drexler

"He's a part of Houston. Just like you see certain sights around here and certain traditions, Hakeem is part of that. The Transco tower, NASA, Hakeem...There are a lot of great players who have been here for a while and done great, but he's Mr. Rocket."

—— Houston Rockets coach Rudy Tomjanovich, on center Hakeem Olajuwon

"IT'S MORE OR LESS COMMON FOR US, NOW. IT'S JUST MARK BEING MARK. HE WAS A FAN BEFORE HE WAS AN OWNER. NOW HE'S DOING THE SAME THINGS AS AN OWNER THAT HE WAS DOING AS A FAN, BUT IT'S JUST GETTING MORE ATTENTION. HE'S THE DENNIS RODMAN OF OWNERS."

—— Dallas Mavericks forward Michael Finley, on controversial owner Mark Cuban, 2001

"HE SHOULD DRESS LIKE A CLOWN BECAUSE HE IS A CLOWN - THAT'S CLOWN BASKETBALL. IT SHOULD BE CLOWN BASKETBALL WHEN IT COMES FROM A CLOWN LIKE DON NELSON.''

—— Los Angeles Lakers center Shaquille O'Neal, frustrated after Dallas Mavericks coach Don Nelson instructed his team to foul the poor free throw shooting center, 2001

"Me and David Stern need to clear our differences. Like I said last night, (let's) just get into a ring. I'll get naked, he'll get naked, and get it on, brother."
—— Dallas Mavericks forward Dennis Rodman, on his on-going differences with NBA commissioner David Stern, 2000

"Mark Cuban wants to win, but he's an owner, not a player. He doesn't need to be hanging round the players like he's a coach or something. That's like Jerry Jones and it's dumb. That's why the Cowboys went down. He needs to be the owner, step back and put people in who can get this team in the right direction."
—— Rodman, after being released by the Dallas Mavericks, on team owner Mark Cuban, 2000

"WHO DOESN'T WANT MORE MONEY? I LOVE BEING A MAVERICK. I LOVE THE CITY OF DALLAS. I LOVE THE FUTURE MARK CUBAN (OWNER) FORESEES WITH THIS TEAM. BUT LOVE DOESN'T PAY THE BILLS."
—— Dallas Mavericks forward Gary Trent, on wanting more money, 2000

"YOU CAN GO TO TWO GAMES FOR THE PRICE OF THE LATEST BOYZ II MEN OR 'N SYNC CD. BOTH ARE ENTERTAINING, BUT WHICH WILL CREATE A MORE LASTING MEMORY?"
—— Cuban, on offering $8 tickets, 2000

"The commissioner feels I broke a rule, and he put me in the slammer. Go to jail. Go directly to jail. Do not pass go."

—— Dallas Mavericks coach Don Nelson, after being fined and suspended by NBA commissioner David Stern for illegally scouting players in Yugoslavia, 2002

"I feel like a kid out of high school. You know how you felt on that first summer day when you didn't have to get up and go to school? That's kind of the way I feel."

—— Nelson, on announcing his retirement during the season (effective immediately), 2005

"I don't know if any of them anticipated this, but they're professionals. This isn't seventh grade and my girlfriend's just left me and she wants her ring back. They know they have a job to do."

—— Cuban, on the Mavericks players' reaction after the surprise announcement that Nelson was retiring immediately

"Ed Rush might have been a great ref, but I wouldn't hire him to run a Dairy Queen."

—— Cuban, on the NBA supervisor of officials. At the fast food diner's invitation, Cuban later worked a day at a DQ in Coppell, Texas. 2002

"THE SUPER BOWL, FROM A TELEVISION PERSPECTIVE, IS THE BIGGEST EVENT OF THE YEAR. BUT FOR ATTENDANCE AND PARTYING, (NBA) ALL-STAR WEEKEND WILL MAKE THE SUPER BOWL LOOK LIKE A BAR MITZVAH."

—— Mark Cuban

"I've had to overcome a lot of diversity."

—— Dallas Mavericks forward Drew Gooden, on his up-and-down career

"I LOOKED LIKE A POSTER CHILD FOR WORLD HUNGER."

—— Houston Rockets reserve center Chuck Nevitt, 7-foot-7 and weighing only 207 pounds

"My sister's expecting a baby, and I don't know if I'm going to be an uncle or an aunt."

—— Nevitt

"I can't really remember the names of the clubs that we went to."

—— NBA center Shaquille O'Neal, when asked if he visited the Parthenon while in Greece

"My kids start pressing as freshmen. We learn early that unless you can play the press and play against the press, you better go see the counselor about transferring to another school in town."

—— Fort Worth Dunbar coach Robert Hughes, on his style of play, 1995

"The worst thing you can do is rush the offense. Because we are a high-octane team, people get the inclination we can't play a half-court game. We can dance fast or slow, it just depends on the partner."

—— Hughes

"ROCKWALL IS LIKE THE TEAM IN THE MOVIE 'HOOSIERS.' THEY'VE GOT ROLE PLAYERS WHO KNOW THEIR ROLE AND DO IT. THEY HAVE SHOOTERS, BALL HANDLERS AND REBOUNDERS, AND THEY PLAY DEFENSE."

—— Texas Hoops magazine publisher Mike Kunstadt, on the 2000 Rockwall High boys' basketball team

"I have seen no team that compares to the '70 and '73 teams. Back in '70, I don't think any Southwest Conference team could have beaten us."

—— Former Houston Wheatley High School coach Jackie Carr, 2001

"Even though we were down by 19 points and bats were flying around on the court, our kids stayed focused. I guess that says a lot about them."

—— Maypearl High coach Jerry Armstrong, after his team lost to Larue La Poyner in the Class 2A state title game. During the game, a small bat flew through the gym. 1995

"PLAYING THEM IS LIKE BEING PUT IN THE WASHING MACHINE AND BEING PUT ON SPIN CYCLE. WE'VE SEEN PRESSURE LIKE THAT, BUT NOT WITH THE SAME ATHLETICISM."

—— Vanderbilt Industrial High School coach Jeff Merchant, after his team lost to Italy, 71-63, in the 1997 Class 2A state championship basketball game

"He had the kind of performance that, to a basketball fan, was awesome, but for the opposing coach, it was just awful. We tried every defense against him, except the bazooka defense, where you take out a gun and shoot him."

—— Lake Highlands High coach Jimmy Roe, after Carrollton Newman Smith's Gordon Alexander scored 47 points against his team, 1995

✫ **10** ✫

WORST TEXAS SPORTS
QUOTES PREDICTIONS/MISJUDGMENTS

1. *"There's only going to be one Grant Teaff for Baylor. But one of the things I said to Dave on his first visit here was, 'You need to consider what Grant did for football and the legacy that he left for our football program. We've never had anyone come in and establish that legacy for basketball. You've got the opportunity to do for Baylor's basketball program what Grant did for football.' And I think he'll do that."* —— Baylor athletic director Tom Stanton, on hiring basketball coach Dave Bliss, 1999 (After four seasons at Baylor, Bliss was forced to resign amidst a scandal that involved the murder of a player and an NCAA investigation.)

2. *"They thought he was too small, a step too slow."* —— Leroy Coleman, LaDainian Tomlinson's high school coach at Waco University High, on why the All-Pro running back wasn't highly recruited by colleges, 2007

3. *"It's not that I didn't like him. But he didn't have stopwatch speed. He was 4.65. He was undersized, had average hands and left school early. Our mistake was we based the decision too much on the numbers and not enough on performance. He's a great player."* —— Tampa Bay personnel director Jerry Angelo, on by-passing future Hall of Fame running back Emmitt Smith in the NFL draft

4. *"When Jerry (Jones) and I talked, we agreed that we were going to Dallas together for our last stop. From the first day I came here, I viewed this as my last job."* —— Jimmy Johnson, 1989 (After winning two Super Bowls in five seasons, Johnson resigned after major disagreements with owner Jerry Jones.)

5. *"I say this without reservation: five years from the time Weltlich takes over, Texas will be nationally competitive. Is that too long? They've been waiting since the beginning of the century."* —— Indiana basketball coach Bob Knight, predicting success for Texas coach Bob Weltlich, 1984 (Weltlich was fired after six years at UT, with a 77-98 record.)

6. *"When we talk about what we're going to be doing this week, next week*

and next year, every bit of that is with the thought that Chan (Gailey) is going to be our coach." — Dallas Cowboys owner Jerry Jones, 2000 (Gailey had a record of 18-14 in two seasons and was fired by Jones in early 2000.)

7. *"He's probably as good as anybody who's ever come along, including Nolan Ryan. He doesn't throw as hard as Nolan did in high school, but he's bigger and stronger. He's progressed further than Nolan at this age."* — Baseball scout Red Murff, on 18-year-old Arlington Martin High School pitcher Todd Van Poppel, 1990 (The hard-throwing pitcher was a first round draft choice of the Oakland Athletics. From 1991-2004, he pitched for seven teams, never winning more than four games in a season. He retired in 2005 with a career record of 40-52.)

8. *"We're a sleeping giant. If we get this thing going, we will turn Fort Worth around. This city is hungry for a winner…What we have to do is win. I promise you that if I don't get this team to the point where we are going to bowl games regularly, the administration won't have to ask me to leave. I couldn't live with myself."* — TCU football coach Pat Sullivan, 1994 (Sullivan resigned after a 1-10 season in 1997. He compiled a record of 24-42-1 in six seasons at TCU.)

9. *"I truly believe North Texas (State) will become a national football power."* — North Texas football coach Hayden Fry, 1973

10. *"I hope that 20 years from now, I can be compared with Darrell (Royal)."* — University of Texas football coach Fred Akers, 1977 (Akers replaced the popular Royal and compiled a record of 86-31-2 from 1977-86. He was fired after the '86 season and later surfaced at Purdue, where he spent four unsuccessful years. By 1997, 20 years after Akers' quote, he was out of the coaching profession.)

"6"

"Now You Chunkin' In There"

Loel Passe was the Norman Vincent Peale of baseball broadcasters. For a generation of fans who grew up with the Houston Colt 45s/Astros in the 1960-70s, radio play-by-play men Gene Elston, sidekick Passe, and Harry Kalas made lasting impressions. And such lasting optimism by Passe was appreciated, as the Houston team (and fans) suffered through many disappointing seasons.

Elston was the straight man, the Joe Friday, "just the facts" guy. Passe (with a silent "e"), with his deep Southern accent, was unabashed in his enthusiasm for the home team. Every year, he picked Houston to win the pennant. One year, he touted a young Astros outfielder as a candidate for rookie of the year; a few weeks later, the youngster was sent to the minors.

Passe teamed with Elston to do Houston games (radio and TV) from 1962-76. One of his signature phrases was delivered when an Astros pitcher was throwing strikes: "Now you chunkin' in there," Loel bellowed over the radio to the pitcher and listeners.

Passe died in 1997 at the age of 80.

"He breezed him, one more time!"

—— Passe, after a strikeout

"Hot ziggity dog and sassafras tea!"
— Passe, after an exciting play

"Now you going in there, gang!"
— Passe, offering encouragement

"HOW ABOUT THEM APPLES?"
— Passe

"HOW aBOUT THEM OranGes?"
— Passe

"CHaIn me TO THE CHaIR."
— Passe

"Peanut butter up and down, jam and jelly all around."
— Passe

"You know, fans, more foul balls are hit into the stands at beautiful Colt Stadium than any other park in the National League."
— Passe

"Every day is Memorial Day at the Astrodome."
— Passe

Now Harry Walker is the one who manages the crew,
He doesn't like it when we drink and fight and smoke and screw,
But when we win our games each day,
Then what the hell can Harry say?

—— Lyrics from "It Makes a Fellow Proud To Be An Astro," sung by players in the early 1970s

"HITTING A BALL TOWARD ROY IS LIKE HITTING IT DOWN A SEWER."

—— Los Angeles Dodgers Wally Moon, on ace Cincinnati shortstop Roy McMillan

"I feel just like I did when I saw the Grand Canyon for the first time."

—— Houston Astros general manager Paul Richards, on seeing the Astrodome for the first time, 1965

"We first walked into the Dome at night and they had it all lit up. I felt like I had walked into a huge flying saucer, like walking into another century."

—— Houston Astros pitcher Larry Dierker

"It's not much, but we call it home."

—— Houston Astros pitcher Jim Owens, when the Astrodome opened in 1965

"FOR ME, THE LOVE AFFAIR WITH THE ASTRODOME ENDED WHEN THEY TOOK DOWN THE SCOREBOARD. FROM THEN ON, IT WAS JUST WAITING UNTIL WE COULD GET A NEW STADIUM."

—— Dierker, 1999

"It used to be that the strength of your team made your reputation as a sports city. Take the Yankees, for instance. But with the Astrodome, it didn't matter that you might have the crappiest team in the nation. People came just to see the Astrodome."

—— Former Houston mayor Fred Hofheinz, 1995

"MISS TAYLOR IS A BEAUTIFUL WOMAN, SURE. BUT HOW DO I KNOW SHE WON'T NAG ME? CAN SHE COOK? CAN SHE HANDLE MONEY? CAN SHE KEEP THE HOUSE NEAT? CAN I TALK BASEBALL WITH HER?"

—— Houston Astros manager Harry Walker, insisting he wouldn't trade his wife for Elizabeth Taylor, 1969

"WE MAY LOSE A LOT, BUT WHEN WE WIN, IT SURE IS DIFFICULT."

—— Houston Astros pitcher Tom Griffin, early 1970s

"I do not want to be the second Clemente. I want to be the first Cedeno."

—— 22-year-old Houston Astros centerfielder Cesar Cedeno, 1973

"The nice thing about Cedeno is that he can play all three outfield positions — at the same time."

—— Montreal Expos manager Gene Mauch

"I don't look for longevity. I look for productivity. If I can escape injury, I should be a fastball pitcher for maybe another five years."

—— California Angels pitcher Nolan Ryan, at age 27, 1974

"I don't picture myself as a junkball pitcher. I've always been a fastball pitcher."

—— Ryan, 1975

"I'd fire my grandmother if I had a chance to get Billy Martin."

—— Texas Rangers owner Bob Short, on firing manager Whitey Herzog and replacing him with Billy Martin, 1973

"HELL, I'D PITCH HITLER IF I THOUGHT HE'D WIN."

—— Billy Martin

"It's been a truthful relationship here with everybody. I have a real foundation here. I think I'll stay here for the rest of my career."

—— Second-year Rangers manager Martin, 1975

"This place is a country club. I'm not allowed to control my players. They want a yes-man here. You can't win ball games if you're a yes-man."

—— Martin, shortly before being fired by Rangers owner Brad Corbett in 1975

"I told him I wasn't tired. He told me, 'No, but the outfielders sure are.'"

—— Texas Rangers pitcher Jim Kern, on the manager who removed him from a game

"We had a very scientific system for bringing in a relief pitcher. We used the first one who answered the bullpen phone."

—— Former Texas Rangers pitching coach Chuck Estrada, during the 1973 season in which Texas had a major league-worst record of 57-105

"The guy is crazy. Having him run a baseball team is like giving a 3-year-old a handful of razor blades."

—— Scout Frank Lane, on Rangers owner Corbett, 1970s

"It's not very often we get to see the Lone Ranger and Toronto the same night."

—— Texas Rangers administrative assistant Bobby Bragan, after a home game against the Toronto Blue Jays and a promotional appearance by Clayton Moore, the original Lone Ranger

"I've always been afraid of success. Right now, I have a fear of my own ego. I don't know of anybody who isn't affected by success, from Jimmy Swaggart to Nolan Ryan. I wonder, will I like success too much? Will I want more fame? More money?"

—— Houston Astros pitcher Bob Knepper, 1988

"HE'S an amazing man. WHEN HE'S aLL THROUGH, THEY BETTER SEND HIS aRM TO THE SMITHSONIAN."

—— Los Angeles Dodgers manager Tommy Lasorda, on pitcher Nolan Ryan, 1989

"People think we make $3 million and $4 million a year. They don't realize that most of us only make $500,000."

—— Texas Rangers outfielder Pete Incaviglia, 1990

"I had certain rules to follow when I was young, and discipline just became a habit. I always wanted to be strong — not just mentally, but physically. I spent many Friday nights when I was at Spring Woods High School running and working out while my friends were out partying and getting drunk."

—— Boston Red Sox pitcher Roger Clemens

"My goals are to hit .300, score 100 runs, and stay injury-prone."

—— Texas Rangers outfielder Mickey Rivers

"THERE'S NO USE GETTING ON ME, BECAUSE I'M NOT GOING TO GET ANY BETTER."

—— Umpire Durwood Merrill, in response to Detroit manager Sparky Anderson arguing a call, 1995

"You talk about a role model — this is a role model. Don't be like me. God gave me the ability to play baseball, and that's what I wanted to do. Gave me everything, and I just wasted it."

—— New York Yankees Hall of Famer Mickey Mantle, after receiving a liver transplant, 1995

"They start to overheat a little bit. They're like one of those turkeys when they're done cooking and the temperature gauge pops out."

—— Texas Rangers coach Bucky Dent, on the rigorous spring training workouts, 1996

"OBVIOUSLY, THAT'S THE PERSONNEL THAT'S VERY LIKELY TO BE ON THE FIELD OPENING DAY, BUT IN WHAT ORDER HAS YET TO BE DETERMINED. IT'S LIKE A TINKER TOY SET — YOU PLAY WITH IT."

—— Texas Rangers manager Johnny Oates, on his spring training lineup, 1996

"It doesn't help when your starting pitcher is up hurling all night."

—— Texas Rangers infielder Mark McLemore, after a 12-3 loss to the Yankees. The night before, several Rangers, including pitcher Kevin Gross, were stricken by food poisoning, 1996

"There are kids growing up in Texas, I'm sure, that want to be like Nolan Ryan or Roger Clemens, and if he continues like this, I'm sure a lot of kids will want to grow up like Kerry Wood."

—— Former major league pitcher David Clyde, on Cubs pitcher Kerry Wood, 1998

"I don't know if Michael Jordan, Bill Gates, Alexander the Great – I don't think anyone is worth this kind of money. But this is the marketplace we're in, it's the money Mr. Hicks chose to pay me and now it's time to go out and pay him back with a few championships."

—— Texas Rangers infielder Alex Rodriguez, after signing a 10-year, $252 million contract with Rangers owner Tom Hicks, 2001

"People in Texas don't have the same baseball tradition as cities in the Northeast. It's only been since air conditioning that this city has been settled. So they don't have a long-standing tradition in anything."

— Former major league pitcher-turned-Astros-broadcaster Joe Sambito, 1999

"He's the Mansion on Turtle Creek and I'm the Country Kitchen on Collins in Arlington."

— Fired Texas Rangers manager Jerry Narron, on his former boss and Rangers general manager John Hart, 2002

"This is a made-for-TV movie. You can't explain why we played so poorly for three months. You can't explain the streak we're in. Just think of the home situation. We have never had good fortune here at home since we opened this ballpark. It's never given us a home-field advantage. All of a sudden we have an unprecedented 18 home wins in a row. It's magic. There's magic in the air."

— Houston Astros general manager Gerry Hunsicker, on Enron Field, which opened in 2000, 2004

"SOMETIMES YOUNG PEOPLE GET SO WRAPPED UP IN WHAT'S GOING ON THAT THEY LOSE SIGHT OF THE BIGGER PICTURE. BUT BRANDON'S BEEN ON A BIG STAGE BEFORE, THOUGH NOT THIS BIG, AS A STARTING QUARTERBACK IN THE HIGH SCHOOL PLAYOFFS IN TEXAS. HE KNOWS SOMETHING ABOUT THIS. HE'S GOTTEN A LITTLE BETTER EACH TIME OUT."

— Houston Astros manager Phil Garner, on starting rookie pitcher Brandon Backe in the first game of the National League Championship Series, 2004

"I don't know of any set of circumstances that we would trade Roger Clemens. Roger is one of the best pitchers in the history of baseball, just as Nolan (Ryan) was. He's a Houston person, a Texan."

—— Astros owner Drayton McLane, on rumors that Houston would trade Clemens to the Texas Rangers, 2005

"I'm frustrated, I'm ticked. I'm animated. I'd like to put on a better show. It's embarrassing to play like this in our hometown. That's some pretty poor hitting, absolute rotten hitting. It's amazing. I don't know how you can win a ballgame when you can't hit the ball. We could have played 40 innings, and it didn't look like we were going to get a runner across the (plate). Very frustrating."

—— Houston Astros manager Phil Garner, after a 14-inning, 7-5 loss to the Chicago White Sox in Game 3 of the 2005 World Series. Houston had only one hit in its final 11 at-bats with runners in scoring position.

"When you're in the bullpen, your role is to pitch. Mark Loretta said it best years ago. You're like a fireman. You come to work and there's not a fire every day, but every once in a while, there's going to be a fire and you've got to go to work and put it out. That's what a bullpen guy does."

—— Garner, 2007

"THEY DON'T HAVE A TOUGHER JOB. IT'S A MORE CREATIVE JOB. IT'S GOING TO BE DIFFERENT. BUT IT'S STILL BASEBALL, NOT ROCKET SCIENCE. I KNOW MORE ABOUT MANAGING IN THE NATIONAL LEAGUE THAN I DO FLYING A ROCKET SHIP TO THE MOON."

—— Rangers manager Johnny Oates, on National League managers and inter-league play

"I'm a hitter who needs lots of maintenance."

—— Houston Astros shortstop Tim Bogar, who was hitting .214, 1997

"I'VE ALWAYS FELT MANAGING IS ONE-TENTH GAME STRATEGY AND NINE-TENTHS PEOPLE SKILLS."

—— Houston Astros manager Larry Dierker

"If you're going to be a good leader, you shouldn't always dictate. It's important to speak your mind, but it's also important to listen."

—— Dierker

"Jesse Owens never got anybody out. I know what I have to do to get myself ready. It's not running."

—— Texas Rangers relief pitcher John Wetteland, on his dislike for running to get into condition in spring training, 1997

"I WORRY ABOUT PRICING OURSELVES OUT OF REACH OF THE TEXAS FAMILY. THAT BASEBALL STADIUM'S GOT TO BE FILLED WITH LITTLE KIDS, HATS ON CROOKED, TRYING TO GET A GLIMPSE OF THEIR FAVORITE BALLPLAYER."

—— Texas Gov. George W. Bush, a part-owner of the Texas Rangers, on the escalating price of sporting events, 1997

"To me, only Nolan Ryan put butts in seats. Maybe a guy like (Sandy) Koufax did, too. But there are only a handful. If you want butts in seats, you win. And winning in this day and age depends largely on how you spread your dollars."

—— Rangers general manager Doug Melvin, on the importance of re-signing catcher Pudge Rodriguez, 1997

"I don't think anybody thought this team was going to be the '27 Yankees. We've taken two All-Stars (Jeff Bagwell and Craig Biggio) and surrounded them with a bunch of average players. That being said, I think this team is clearly capable of playing much better than we have."

—— Astros general manager Gerry Hunsicker, on his second place team's 43-45 record at the All-Star break, 1997

"WHAT'S HE GOING TO DO, ARM-TACKLE ME? HE'S BASICALLY JUST A GLORIFIED FLAG-FOOTBALL PLAYER WHO CAN RUN."

—— Philadelphia Phillies pitcher Curt Schilling, on throwing inside in his on-going feud with Deion Sanders, 1997

"Now I know what a lot of rock stars feel like."

—— New Houston Astros pitcher Randy Johnson, after receiving a standing ovation in the Astrodome, 1998

"IF CLEMENS STAYS WITH US, IT'S NOT A BAD SITUATION TO BE IN. HE HAS DEMANDED A TRADE, BUT IT DEPENDS ON THE OFFERS WE GET. WE'RE NOT TRADING HIM FOR TWO CANS OF DIET COKE."

—— Toronto Blue Jays general manager Gord Ash, on the prospects of trading Cy Young winner Roger Clemens, 1998

"we don't need a canadian lecturing texans on their duty to their home state."

—— Randy Hendricks, Roger Clemens' agent, on Texas Rangers GM Doug Melvin (a Canadian native) complaining about Clemens signing a free agent contract with New York, 1999

"The catcher is much like a quarterback in football. You can't just do it on raw physical talent. You've got to have brains. The catcher makes more decisions during a ballgame than a manager does."

—— Rangers manager Johnny Oates

"We are surprised and disappointed that he is going to be so late. Pudge wants to be a Hall of Famer, and he talks about that a lot. I wonder how often Johnny Bench was late for spring training. My guess is not very often. Pudge has started making being late a routine."

—— Texas Rangers general manager Doug Melvin, on Pudge Rodriguez reporting late to camp, 1999

"He didn't have to make a comparison. I'm Ivan Rodríguez. I'm a catcher. Johnny Bench is Johnny Bench. Doug said that wrong. I think they don't remember for seven years I reported early and now I show up a week late, and he's going to come with this? It's not right. I'm real mad about it."

—— Rodriguez

"I DON'T CONSIDER MYSELF A LEADER."

—— Rodriguez

141

"If you're the President of the United States, if you're the owner of the Dallas Stars or if you're an All-Star catcher, you're going to be a leader. The only question is what kind of a leader you want to be. If you're a multi-Gold Glove winner, you're looked up to. You don't have any choice about that. In two years, we're probably not going to remember that Pudge showed up late for camp this year. We're just disappointed in it."

—— Rangers manager Oates

"I don't believe in a sophomore jinx. Anybody can have a slump. No matter what year it is. When Frank Thomas has a slump, is it a grad school jinx?"

—— Oakland A's outfielder Ben Grieve, the 1998 AL rookie of the year, 1999

"Hello, win column!"

—— Longtime Texas Rangers play-by-play announcer Mark Holtz, after a win

"I DON'T KNOW IF THERE IS ANY (BAD BLOOD) BETWEEN THE TEAMS OR NOT, BUT I KNOW I DON'T LIKE THEM."

—— TCU coach Lance Brown, after a confrontation with the University of Texas baseball team, 1996

"I honestly prefer the home run because there's less teaching involved. They hit it and then really all they have to do is touch all the bases."

—— University of Texas coach Augie Garrido, 2000

"THE YANKEES WOULDN'T HIT FOR HOME RUNS IN DISCH-FALK FIELD. WE'VE GOT POWER. WE JUST PLAY IN THE GRAND CANYON."

—— Garrido

"WHEN HE HIT THE HOME RUN, I THANKED HIM AND HIS MOTHER AND FATHER AND THEIR MOTHERS AND FATHERS AND ANYBODY WHO HAD ANYTHING TO DO WITH CHANCE BEING ON THIS PLANET."

—— Garrido, after Chance Wheeless' game-winning homer defeated Baylor in the College World Series, sending UT to the championship series, 2005

"Baseball had always been my best sport. I didn't consider myself a good football player in high school. I always wanted to be a pro baseball player as a kid."

—— Hall of Fame quarterback Sammy Baugh, 1998

"We're fortunate in that we've probably got a pitching staff that is better than a lot of college teams."

—— Boswell High School coach David Hatcher, during the 1997 playoffs

"We've been playing in it a long time, but my butt's sore from getting it kicked all weekend. The person that schedules us in that tourney is an idiot. And since that's me, I've made the decision we won't be going next year."

—— Fort Worth Eastern Hills High coach Derek Matlock, after his highly- touted team lost three of five games in an Austin tournament that came after district play started, 1997

"I'M ALWAYS LIKE, 'MAN, PUT ME OUT THERE. I CAN DO JUST AS BAD AS THOSE GUYS. I CAN GO OUT THERE AND GIVE UP RUNS.' I THINK I'M GONNA MOVE UP QUICK, AND I'M GONNA CHANGE THAT 'ERA AROUND. HOPEFULLY THEY'LL COME TO THEIR SENSES AND REALIZE WHAT THEY'RE GETTING."

—— Irving High pitcher Blake Beavan, shortly after being drafted in the first round by the Texas Rangers, 2007

✮ **10** ✮

FORGOTTEN OR UNDERRATED
TEXAS SPORTS QUOTABLE FIGURES

1. **Dick Motta**
2. **Shelby Metcalf**
3. **Billy Tubbs**
4. **Jimmy Demaret**
5. **Mickey Rivers**
6. **Jim Wacker**
7. **Bobby Layne**
8. **Bill Peterson**
9. **Jerry Glanville**
10. **Kern Tips**

"7"

"The Behinder We Got, The Worser It Got"

Oail Andrew "Bum" Phillips certainly paid his dues, coming up through the coaching ranks to eventually lead two National Football League franchises – the Houston Oilers and New Orleans Saints.

After stints at a number of Texas high schools and one year as an assistant at Texas A&M (under Bear Bryant), Phillips became head coach at Texas Western (now UTEP). A year later, he began the life of a journeyman assistant, serving in that role at the University of Houston, SMU, Oklahoma State, and in the NFL with the San Diego Chargers and Houston Oilers.

Finally, in 1975, Phillips was named head coach and general manager of the Oilers, serving in that capacity through 1980. He was quite the folk hero, delighting the "Luv Ya Blue" fans with his tobacco-chewing, beer-drinking, "good old boy" ways. In addition, the players responded to his laid-back, blue-collar approach to the game. At games, Phillips hid his crew cut by wearing a cowboy hat (except in the Astrodome) and sported a western shirt, jeans/slacks and boots. During this time, the Oilers and Phillips were the antithesis to the Dallas Cowboys and their coach, Tom Landry. Dallas — known as "America's Team" — was the slick, glitzy squad whose coach wore tailored suits and a fedora.

Phillips, the winningest coach in franchise history, led the Oilers to two American Football Conference championship games. Phillips' plain-speaking manner was a hit with the press, and his countrified, philosophical quotes were often quite colorful.

Bum and son Wade Phillips coached together for several years; Bum retired as the Saints coach in 1985, and Wade is now head coach of the Dallas Cowboys.

Perhaps Bum Phillips is the closest thing we have to the late Dizzy Dean, the renowned baseball-pitcher-turned-broadcaster, who infuriated English teachers everywhere with his sub-par grammar skills.

For example, after falling behind early to the rival Pittsburgh Steelers in a 1979 playoff game, Bum drawled, "the behinder we got, the worser it got."

"Shula can take his'n and beat your'n, or he can take your'n and beat his'n."
— Phillips, on the success of NFL coach Don Shula

"BEFORE THE GAME, I THOUGHT WE WERE IN A GOOD FRAME OF MIND. BUT HELL, YOU CAN'T STOP NOBODY WITH A FRAME OF MIND."
— Phillips

"He's wide and slung low. He's just like one of those old cement irrigation tanks."
— Phillips, describing a player

"I'D RATHER HAVE A GOOD HIGH SCHOOL COACHING JOB THAN A LOUSY PRO COACHING JOB."
— Phillips

"I'D RATHER BE COACH OF THE HOUSTON OILERS THAN PRESIDENT OF THE UNITED STATES."

—— Phillips

"You can't worry in this business. There are only two kinds of coaches: those who have been fired and those who are gonna be fired."

—— Phillips

"I don't think Billy Graham could have brought us back."

—— Phillips, on his team trailing 31-3 at the half

"This year I said the road to the Super Bowl went through Pittsburgh. I'll tell you one damn thing – next year the road to the Super Bowl goes through Houston. One year ago we knocked on the door. This year we beat on the door. Next year we're gonna kick the son-of-a-bitch in."

—— Phillips, to Oilers fans at a welcome home rally in the Astrodome after his team lost to Pittsburgh in the 1979 AFC Championship Game

"If they're America's team, we must be Texas's team."

—— Phillips, after beating the Dallas Cowboys

"IF PRACTICE WASN'T IMPORTANT, WE WOULDN'T HAVE IT. WE'D PLAY ON SUNDAYS AND TAKE THE REST OF THE WEEK OFF."

—— Phillips

"Even old football coaches need love."

—— Phillips

"It reminds me of a good three-wood lie."

—— Pro golfer Carol Mann, on Bum Phillips's crew cut

"Hell, we pardon murderers in this country. Surely to goodness you can give a football player a second chance."

—— Phillips, on giving a troubled player a second chance

"I AIN'T DOING A DAMN THING, AND I DON'T START UNTIL NOON."

—— Phillips, on how he's spending his retirement time, 1988

"I've always said these things. Only when I was at Nederland High School, people weren't coming around and asking me questions."

—— Phillips

"I THINK SAMMY BAUGH WAS THE GREATEST (QUARTERBACK) OF ALL TIME, AND NOT JUST BECAUSE HE WAS A TEXAN. SAM COULD THROW THE BALL BETTER THAN ANYONE I EVER SAW."

—— Hall of Fame quarterback Bobby Layne, 1962

"WITH GOOD PROTECTION AND THE CONFIDENCE OF YOUR TEAM, A QUARTERBACK SHOULD HAVE NO TROUBLE PLAYING UNTIL HE'S 40 YEARS OLD."

—— Layne

"When a new player reports to the team, I never look at his build, his eyes or anything like that. I just stare at his feet. Nobody can run fast with big feet, and besides, they look bad."

—— Layne

"I'm not going to talk about leaving because the people of Houston would think I was bluffing. I haven't made up my mind, anyhow...Maybe if we can get the Rams and other NFL clubs playing here, the attendance will pick up."

—— Houston Oilers owner Bud Adams, 1967

"We have 12 Texans on this team. They were hand-picked because they're tough. They grow them tough in Texas. We like tough football players."

—— Green Bay Packers coach Vince Lombardi, after his team beat Dallas in the NFL Championship Ice Bowl, 1967

"If I can't outrun someone named Martha, I shouldn't be in this league."

—— Dallas Cowboys receiver Pete Gent, after outrunning Pittsburgh Steelers defensive back Paul Martha to score a TD

"HE HAS LEADERSHIP QUALITIES YOU MAY FIND ONCE IN 10 MILLION MEN. PEOPLE GET A KICK OUT OF BEING AROUND HIM."

—— Dallas Cowboys tackle Ralph Neely, on teammate and quarterback Don Meredith, 1968

"I believe Meredith was the greatest quarterback Dallas ever had, including Staubach...Don Meredith was simply one of the greatest natural-born leaders ever to play football. As far as knowing the game and knowing how to lead men, nobody could touch Meredith."
— Former Dallas Cowboys fullback Walt Garrison

"Well, we know we'll never make Don Meredith into Bart Starr. They're different personalities...Meredith is like a Babe Ruth or a Bobby Layne. If Starr is Stan Musial, Meredith is Mickey Mantle. I understand that, but sometimes I get annoyed at his flippancy."
— Dallas Cowboys president-general manager Tex Schramm, 1968

"ONCE, I WAS SITTING ON THIS PLANE AND JUST DECIDED I DIDN'T WANT TO PLAY FOOTBALL ANYMORE...I CAN'T EXPLAIN WHY. I JUST KNEW IT WAS TIME TO QUIT. THE SAME THING HAPPENED WHEN I LEFT 'MONDAY NIGHT FOOTBALL.' I JUST KNEW IT WAS TIME."
— Meredith, 1998

"I don't miss the limelight. I'm just more comfortable out of it. Dandy Don is somebody else. He wasn't a bad guy. I have great memories, but I don't miss any of it."
— Meredith

"He was the guy who really started the franchise. He put the position of quarterback on the map. He's the pioneer to Staubach, Aikman, and the guys after them. It's kind of neat to have a club like that — such great players and it all started with him."

—— Dallas Cowboys quarterback Tony Romo, on his respect for Don Meredith, 2007

"Evidently."

—— Dallas Cowboys running back Duane Thomas, when asked after the team's Super Bowl VI win if he was fast. Thomas did not speak to the media or his teammates during the entire season.

"THE COWBOYS WERE IN THE SUPER BOWL LAST SEASON, AND I DIDN'T SEE THEM GRADUATING ANY SENIORS."

—— Philadelphia Eagles coach Dick Vermeil, newly arrived from UCLA, on why Dallas was the league favorite, 1976

"THERE IS NOT A BIG DEMAND FOR A 210-POUND CENTER WHO ORGANIZES UNIONS."

—— Bill Curry, Houston Oilers center and president of the NFL Players Association, on why he hadn't received an offer from the World Football League, 1974

"Anybody can have an off decade."

—— Dallas Cowboys defensive lineman Larry Cole, who scored three touchdowns in 1968-69 on fumbles and interceptions, and not another one until 1980

"We don't carry an 'S' on our chest. We just wear a star on our helmet and try to do the best job we can."

—— Dallas Cowboys running back Emmitt Smith, after rushing for just 69 yards in a season-opening 37-7 win over Pittsburgh, 1997

"As a player, I detested Tom Landry. He was so mechanical and distant. I left the Dallas Cowboys in 1974 after five years, in part to escape his suffocating ethic."

—— Former Cowboys lineman Pat Toomay, 2000

"I don't think Coach Landry should be judged on the number of games he won. He should be judged on the number of lives he influenced. He had a higher winning percentage doing that than winning games."

—— Former Cowboys safety Charlie Waters

"IT'S THE END OF AN ERA, OUR ERA. A LOT OF OLD COWBOYS ARE CRYING TONIGHT."

—— Former Cowboys defensive lineman Bob Lilly, on the firing of Tom Landry, 1989

"Jerry (Jones) is a great boss to work for. It's like one of those assistant coaches said the other night: When Jimmy Johnson gets another job out there, he's going to find out there's a hell of a lot worse owners to work for in this league than Jerry Jones."

—— Dallas Cowboys coach Barry Switzer, on his predecessor, Jimmy Johnson

"It took me five years to put the team together. We'll see what happens with Barry Switzer."

—— Former Cowboys coach Jimmy Johnson

"THOSE GUYS KNOW WHO THE BOSS IS. THEY KNOW THEY WORK FOR ME. I MAKE THE CALL ON THE COACHES. JERRY (JONES) AND I DISCUSSED THAT. THEY KNOW THAT. THEY KNOW HOW I WORK, HOW THE SYSTEM WORKS. JUST BECAUSE I HAVE A SMILE ON MY FACE, AND I'M MORE FUN TO WORK WITH AND BE AROUND DOESN'T MEAN I CAN'T FIRE OR HIRE ANYBODY. I'VE DONE THAT BEFORE. I'VE ONLY DONE IT WHEN NECESSARY."

—— Switzer

"We all do things differently as coaches. Tom Landry coached them from his tower. Jimmy Johnson coached from a distance. I want to be in there close to where I can feel the heartbeat and the pulse of the football team."

—— Switzer

"IT'S FUN WHEN YOU GO TO THE FAT STOCK SHOW AND EVERYBODY PETS THOSE PRETTY MARES. AND IF YOU HAVE SOME OLD, SKINNY STOCK OVER THERE, THEY DON'T GET MUCH ATTENTION. SO, WE'RE THE OLD, SKINNY ONES RIGHT NOW."

—— Houston Oilers coach Jack Pardee, on his 1-5 team, 1994

"Dallas puts you in a situation where it is almost like minimum wage, like 10 or 15 years from now you have your kids asking, 'Well, why can't you afford to send me to college, Dad?' And I would have to say, 'Well, I decided to play for the Cowboys instead of the 49ers.' "

—— Former Cowboys linebacker Ken Norton, Jr., who signed a five-year, $8 million free-agent pact with the 49ers, 1995

"I watched 'Rudy' this morning, 'Field of Dreams' last night, and Jason in between."

—— Switzer, on young quarterback Jason Garrett's remarkable performance against the Green Bay Packers

"YOU CAN STICK IOWA STATE UP YOUR ASS."

—— Cincinnati Bengals coach David Shula, to Switzer at midfield after losing to Dallas, 23-20. Earlier in the week, Switzer had compared the winless Bengals to Iowa State.

"They could play this game in Corsicana, in the rain or in the snow, and it wouldn't matter. Emotions will be riding high. It's going to be a great collision."

—— Cowboys cornerback Kevin Smith, on the Dallas-San Francisco NFL championship game, 1995

"We don't let our egos get in the way of the ball club. We understand that sometimes you have to suppress your own selfish desires to benefit the team. Maybe that is something Jimmy and Jerry never understood and were never capable of understanding."

—— Dallas Cowboys quarterback Troy Aikman, 1994

"YOU CAN TALK ABOUT DEION, HIS MAMA, HIS DADDY, HIS WIFE AND HIS KIDS, BUT DON'T SAY A THING ABOUT THE DEFENSE."

—— Cowboys defensive back Deion Sanders, after a 20-17 loss to Philadelphia

"(Deion) Sanders couldn't tackle my wife Emma."

—— Former NFL linebacker Chuck Bednarik, 1996

"The fat lady has sung. She's on the way in the limo back to the hotel with us."

—— Sanders, after the team's 27-17 win over Pittsburgh in Super Bowl XXX, 1996

"There is just no need to have longer agreements or extended obligations unless it is necessary to get the job done. But I want to reiterate that apart from doing the right thing financially for the club, my personal feelings are that he will be coaching the Dallas Cowboys for many years to come."

—— Cowboys owner Jerry Jones, on Switzer, 1996

"You have a few good friends you can count on. The rest of the people who criticize you or don't like (you), they're all molecules in the spectrum of the universe. I don't care that much what people think anymore."

—— Switzer, on criticism, 1996

"I'm not gonna drink RC Cola and double-date with him (Troy Aikman)."
—— Switzer, on his strained relationship with quarterback Aikman, 1996

"IT'S NOT HARD TO BE A FOOTBALL COACH. IT'S OVERRATED. YOU PEOPLE (THE MEDIA) MAKE GURUS AND MYTHS OUT OF THESE PEOPLE, AND THEN THE GUYS START TO BELIEVE IT. THAT'S YOUR FAULT."

—— Switzer, 1996

"I know they're ignorant. My critics are people that haven't spent 35 years doing what my coaches have done. It's like having a bus driver be a critic for an English or history professor."
— Switzer, on critics, 1996

"Hollywood was sort of an alter-ego of drug addiction and women. Hollywood never played football. He was hanging out with Marvin Gaye and doing wild things."
— Former Dallas linebacker Thomas "Hollywood" Henderson, 2000

"...I'M VERY GLAD I DIDN'T HAVE TO PLAY PROFESSIONALLY IN DALLAS. REALITY IS SO FAR-FETCHED FROM WHAT COWBOYS PLAYERS BELIEVE...MOST NFL PLAYERS ARE PUT ON A PEDESTAL. COWBOYS ARE PUT SO HIGH, IT SEEMS LIKE THEY ARE ON ANOTHER PLANET."
— Former SMU and New England Patriots running back Craig James, on Dallas Cowboys players' off-the-field problems, 1996

"If I was Jerry Jones, I'd have an entire wing at Betty Ford (treatment center) just for the Cowboys. I think history tells us it has been a team that needs an entire wing."
— "Hollywood" Henderson, 1997

"WHAT DO YOU WANT ME TO DO, TAKE HIM OUT AND SHOOT HIM?"
— Switzer, when asked what he would do about running back Sherman Williams' problem of fumbling. Earlier that same day, Switzer pled guilty to a misdemeanor charge of carrying a gun without a permit. 1997

"It probably would have been best if I had encouraged Barry (Switzer) to leave after we won the Super Bowl. But he never got credit for the job he did."
— Cowboys owner Jerry Jones, 1999

"I had two good years in Dallas. We'll leave it at that."
— Former Dallas Cowboys coach Chan Gailey, after being named offensive coordinator of the Miami Dolphins, 2000

"I'M EXCITED ABOUT CREATING THE CAPACITY. I WANT 100,000 SEATS. I WANT THIS TO BE A VENUE THAT SPEAKS FOR WHAT THE COWBOYS ARE. WE HAVE THE FRANCHISE THAT BOTH NATIONALLY AND INTERNATIONALLY CAN BE IDENTIFIED WITH THE COLISEUM OF ROME."
— Jones, on the concept of his new stadium, 2000 (Cowboys Stadium opened in 2009.)

"THAT IS ALL I HAVE TO SAY, WARDEN. OH, I WOULD LIKE TO SAY IN CLOSING – WHAT ABOUT THOSE COWBOYS!"
— Inmate William Davis' last words before he was executed in Huntsville, 2000

"My relationship with the Cowboys hasn't been good. You have to admire the way they brought in the talent to win the Super Bowls. Getting Jimmy (Johnson) was a big key. If Tom (Landry) had retired, Jimmy would have been one of my top picks."
— Former Dallas Cowboys president-general manager Tex Schramm, 1999

"Troy (Aikman) will always be a Dallas Cowboy. When people look at him, they will always see him with a star on the side of his helmet."
— Cowboys owner Jerry Jones, 2001

"I was the last one (of the Triplets) to come, but that doesn't mean I had to be the last one to go. That's not the way I would have written the script. I would have written a happy ending. You know, most stories about Cowboys have happy endings."
—— Emmitt Smith, when Dallas released Troy Aikman, 2001

"The quarterback is in charge of the chuck wagon. He's handing it out here and there, but he can't just throw it out there indiscriminately or the wolves will get him."
—— Dallas Cowboys coach Bill Parcells, 2004

"I don't like celebrity quarterbacks. We don't need those. We need battlefield commanders."
—— Parcells

"IF YOU ARE A STAR ON THIS TEAM IN DALLAS, TEXAS, IT'S LIKE BEING TOM CRUISE OR LEONARDO DICAPRIO IN LOS ANGELES. YOU CAN OWN THE TOWN. OF COURSE, IT CAN BE A BLESSING OR A CURSE."
—— Former Cowboys receiver Michael Irvin, on rookie star running back Julius Jones, 2004

"He's thick, but he has to lose a little weight. We're not playing Chubby Checker out there. I know what his former coach had him play at, so we're going with that."
—— Parcells, on rookie defensive tackle Marcus Spears, 2005

"I know we get along well. We're making decisions in a healthy way with good debate, and all of that is working a lot better than most people thought it would."

— Jerry Jones, on his relationship with Parcells, 2005

"YOU GET A LITTLE DOWN AND OUT ONCE IN A WHILE, BUT I DIDN'T THINK ABOUT QUITTING. I DIDN'T THINK ABOUT QUITTING. I JUST WOULDN'T DO IT."

— Parcells, recalling the tough 2004 season

"Don't put him in Canton yet."

— Parcells, after an outstanding pre-season game performance by rookie DeMarcus Ware, 2005

"IT'S a very easy thing to say, 'go get a backup quarterback,' or 'Dallas is caught without a backup quarterback.' right. now tell me where to get them. you can't just dial them up. you cannot. you have these names, some of these guys that are out of work and it's, 'just go get so and so.' well, you don't know what shape so and so is in. you don't know if he can throw it. you don't know if he's playing softball for somebody down at the fire station."

— Parcells, on the difficulty of finding a backup QB in the NFL, 2005

"THE KID WILL RUN. HE WILL BLOCK. HE WILL CATCH. I'M NOT SAYING HE'S GOING TO BE GALE SAYERS. BUT HE HAS ABILITY IN ALL THE AREAS THAT ARE PREREQUISITES."

— Parcells, on rookie running back Marion Barber, who rushed for 127 yards and two touchdowns in a 34-13 win over Arizona, 2005

"Terrell has 25 million reasons why he should be alive."
—— Kim Etheredge, Dallas Cowboys receiver Terrell Owens' publicist, denying a report that Owens had attempted suicide, 2006

"He's a wolf in sheep's clothing. His competitiveness, his will, his wanting to prove that his skills can make a world champion -- that's why I hired him."
—— Dallas Cowboys owner Jerry Jones, on first-year Dallas coach Wade Phillips, 2007

"But we've just played three games. I told the players this is 19 percent of our season, if my math is right, which it usually is. It's only 19 percent. Eighty-one percent is left. You are not measured on 19 percent. You are measured on the whole season."
—— Phillips, telling his 3-0 team that they had 81 percent of the season still to go, 2007

"I wasn't partying with her, that's for sure. She's a nice girl, though."
—— Dallas quarterback Tony Romo, on media reports that he had crossed paths with troubled pop star Britney Spears at a trendy Hollywood club, 2007

"Now Tony has two things to be careful with — the football and his money. Both are equally hard to take care of, and there's always someone out there trying to strip you of them. I hope he hangs on tight. The circus never stays in town forever."
—— Former Dallas coach Bill Parcells, on Romo's new $67.5 million contract, 2007

"IT IS A FEEL-GOOD STORY. THE BEST PART OF THE STORY IS HE'S A GREAT PERSON, A GREAT GUY TO BE AROUND. HE DOESN'T HAVE AN EGO BIGGER THAN THE TEAM. THE GREAT ONES I'VE BEEN AROUND — THE JOHN ELWAYS, THE JIM KELLYS — IT'S THE SAME WAY."

— Cowboys coach Wade Phillips, on Romo's new contract, 2007

"I'm still waiting for some cute girl to say, 'You're rich; let's hang out.' But it still hasn't happened."

— Romo, joking about his new $67.5 million contract

"YOU MEAN HE'S THAT GOOD-LOOKING?"

— Legendary Cowboys quarterback Don Meredith, when told that a lot of fans were comparing Dallas quarterback Tony Romo to a young Meredith, 2007

"RIGHT NOW, JESSICA SIMPSON IS NOT A FAN FAVORITE IN THIS LOCKER ROOM OR IN TEXAS STADIUM. I THINK WITH EVERYTHING THAT HAS HAPPENED, AND OBVIOUSLY THE WAY TONY PLAYED AND THE COMPARISON BETWEEN HER AND CARRIE UNDERWOOD, I THINK A LOT OF PEOPLE FEEL LIKE SHE'S KIND OF TAKEN HIS FOCUS AWAY. NO, I'M NOT TRYING TO BE A DISTRACTION. I UNDERSTAND HOW EVERYBODY IS LOOKING AT JESSICA SIMPSON AS A DISTRACTION AND THAT'S DEFINITELY NOT HOW I SAW IT. THAT'S HOW THE MEDIA SAW IT. IF ANYBODY WANTS TO LOOK AT IT AS A NEGATIVE, THEY CAN DO THAT. BUT FOR ME, SHE WAS THERE TO SUPPORT TONY. HE HAD A BAD GAME. I DON'T THINK SHE HAD ANYTHING TO DO WITH IT. WE LOST AS A TEAM. I TRIED TO GET (ROMO) TO CALL HER SO I CAN EXPLAIN TO HER THAT SHE REALLY DOESN'T KNOW ME AND THAT I CAN BE FUNNY, AND THAT EVERYTHING I SAY, THE MEDIA WILL TAKE IT AND RUN WITH IT. IT'S NOT A BIG DEAL. I WILL TRY TO RECTIFY THE SITUATION BETWEEN HER AND I. MAN, I WAS JOKING, EVERYONE WAS LAUGHING, RIGHT?"

— Terrell Owens, 2007

"I don't know if he's the next 'American Idol.' But he played really well."

—— Wade Phillips, on Romo's performance against Green Bay

"THIS IS NOT ABOUT TONY. YOU GUYS CAN POINT THE FINGER AT HIM, YOU CAN TALK ABOUT THE VACATION, AND IF YOU DO THAT, IT'S REALLY UNFAIR. IT'S REALLY UNFAIR. THAT'S MY TEAMMATE. THAT'S MY QUARTERBACK. YOU GUYS DO THAT, IT'S NOT FAIR. WE LOST AS A TEAM. WE LOST AS A TEAM, MAN."

—— Owens, after a 21-17 playoff loss to the New York Giants, 2008

"I'm content in my own skin. I feel like I'm doing it the right way. When I made the choice to do those things, I thought I was making good decisions like not going to Vegas and drinking for two or three days."

—— Romo, after the loss and about the trip to Mexico with girlfriend Jessica Simpson

"I think he does, but every good quarterback needs a backup."

—— Former Dallas quarterback Roger Staubach, when asked by real estate icon Ebby Halliday if current Cowboys QB Tony Romo had a girlfriend, 2008

"He just wants to win and be a great player. It's not really all that different than most any guy in here really. He's just more vocal once in a while."

—— Romo, on Terrell Owens

"THE DEMISE OF TERRELL OWENS WAS GREATLY EXAGGERATED."

— Wade Phillips, after Owens caught seven passes for 213 yards in a win over San Francisco, 2008

"He can play with that injured toe. He can play with the soreness and a combination of those things. I see nothing that led us to believe he couldn't."

—— Cowboys owner Jerry Jones, expressing his surprise that injured (dislocated toe) fullback Marion Barber did not suit up for a crucial game (and loss) in Pittsburgh, 2008

"Jimmy (Johnson) was 1-15. Bill (Parcells) had rough years and didn't get fired. The coaches don't get fired for necessarily losing. They can get fired when they're winning Super Bowls, if we've got any humor in us."

—— Jones, denying rumors that he was going to fire coach Wade Phillips, 2008

"I WAKE UP TOMORROW AND KEEP LIVING. YOU JUST KEEP PLAYING THE GAME. I'VE HAD A LOT WORSE HAPPEN TO ME THAN A LOSS IN A SPORTING EVENT, THAT'S FOR SURE, AND IF THIS IS THE WORST THING THAT EVER HAPPENS TO ME, THEN I'VE LIVED A PRETTY GOOD LIFE."

—— Romo, after a disappointing regular season-ending 44-6 loss to Philadelphia that knocked Dallas out of the playoffs, 2008

"This is obviously very disappointing right now, but we won't have a head coaching change."

—— Jones, after the loss to Philadelphia, on speculation that he would fire coach Wade Phillips, 2008

"I'm a football coach. I'm obviously not an orator or a media darling, but I'm a football coach."
—— Phillips

"I THINK BEING aS rOMO-FrIENDLY aS OUr TEaM CaN BE. rOMO-FrIENDLY MEaNS LET'S UTILIZE HIS SKILLS TO THE FULLEST aND MaKE SUrE EVErYTHING WE DO MaXIMIZES HIS aBILITIES."
—— Jones, on quarterback Tony Romo and shortly before controversial wide receiver Terrell Owens was released in 2009

"THERE'S a FINE LINE, THOUGH. WE NEED TO ENJOY IT, BUT EVERYONE'S GOING TO BE DRINKING THE COWBOY KOOL-aID HERE aND TELLING US HOW GREaT WE aRE aND HOW GOOD WE'RE DOING. WE HaVE a LONG WaY TO GO aND a LOT OF FOOTBaLL TO PLaY. aS LONG aS WE PREPaRE THE WaY WE'VE BEEN PREPaRING aND COME OUT ON THE FIELD WITH CONFIDENCE ON SUNDaY, WE'RE GOING TO BE RIGHT WHERE WE WaNT TO BE."
—— Dallas Cowboys linebacker Keith Brooking, on the team's early season success, 2009

"Kraft Macaroni & Cheese is excited about the possibility of working with the city of Irving, Texas, to be involved in the explosion of Texas Stadium."
—— Joanne Freed, a public relations executive, announcing that the company would be sponsoring the implosion of Texas Stadium in 2010

166

★ **10** ★

ALL-TIME BEST
TEXAS SPORTS QUOTES

1. *"Adolph Hitler wore a coat and tie. I don't think that made him a nice guy."* — University of Texas basketball coach Abe Lemons, on his disdain for dress codes

2. *"You can make a lot of money in this game. Just ask my ex-wives. Both of them are so rich that neither of their husbands work."* — Pro golfer Lee Trevino

3. *"He treats us like men. He lets us wear earrings."* — Houston Cougars receiver Torrin Polk, on coach John Jenkins

4. *"The only time Jimmy Johnson didn't run up the score was 27 years ago when he took the SAT."* — CBS-TV sportscaster Jim Nantz, on football coach Jimmy Johnson

5. *"Someone asked me if I was a Phi Beta Kappa once, and I said, 'Naw, I'm a Pisces.'"* — Texas Tech football coach Spike Dykes

6. *"Baylor is like everybody else. You beat Texas and it makes your year. It's too bad Baptists don't drink in public. It would be a nice night for them to celebrate."* — Lemons, after an upset loss to Baylor

7. *"Our strong safety hurt his shoulder in the locker room raising his arm to say 'Charge.'"* — Texas-El Paso football coach Bill Yung, on how bad things had gone for his team in 1983

8. *"There are certain special things in this world, and right at the top are drivers and wives. I know. I've had three of each."* — Trevino

9. *"Sure. Back in McKinney on those cameras they have in Gibson's store to see if you're stealing anything."* — Texas Tech running back Sam Bailey, appearing on Tech coach Steve Sloan's TV show, when asked if he had been on TV before

10. *"Now, I lay me down to sleep."* — Houston Oilers coach Bill Peterson, leading his team in what he meant to be The Lord's Prayer

"8"

"A Pirate Can Beat A Soldier —
The Final Chapter"

You can add acting to the list of credits on Mike Leach's resume, which also includes coaching, radio/TV sports analysis, and law school, among many other historical pursuits.

In Fall 2009, then-Texas Tech coach Leach made a cameo appearance on the critically-acclaimed TV show, "Friday Night Lights."

The show depicts the importance of high school football in fictional Dillon, Texas, and is loosely based on the best-selling book of the same title by H.G. Bissinger.

Other coaches making guest appearances on previous episodes were Mack Brown (player's dad) and Rick Barnes (college football recruiter) of the University of Texas.

Leach told the *Lubbock Avalanche-Journal* that he was allowed to provide input to the show's writers.

"It was kind of scripted and then it was kind of, 'Well, here's the scenario, do what you want,' " Leach said in the A-J article. "Include this, this, this and this.' Actually, in the original (filming), there's stuff about Napoleon, Daniel Boone, grizzly bears, raccoons, a bunch of stuff. We covered

169

a lot of bases, and they picked from what they wanted."

The scene was taped at a gas station outside Austin the night before Tech played Texas in September 2009. In it, Leach pulls up to a gas pump and asks the customer at the next bay directions to Lubbock. There's a hint of recognition as Leach realizes he's pulled alongside the despondent coach of downtrodden East Dillon High School.

The conversation between Leach's character and East Dillon coach Eric Taylor (played by Kyle Chandler) goes like this:

Leach: "Hey, do you know how to get to Lubbock?"

Coach Taylor: "You gotta take 61 up to 23."

Leach: "Hey, Dillon East, right? You're the coach at Dillon East. You've lost your inner pirate. Uh, have you ever heard 'swing your sword'? You're supposed to swing your sword like this, but you're swinging yours like this. You've got to find your inner pirate. A lot of times things just happen for a reason. We don't know why God wants it that way, but you can't make the best out of it until you get back your inner pirate. You might be the luckiest man alive and not even know it."

After delivering his message and filling his gas tank, Leach climbs into his SUV and drives off, leaving Coach Taylor with a somewhat bewildered look on his face.

The scene lasts about a minute.

According to the A-J, there was at least one take left on the cutting-room floor: Leach said he grabbed a burrito out of Taylor's hand and tossed it away to get the coach's attention. Actually, Leach said in the filming they "loaded him up with burritos," and Leach pulled one away from the coach during several takes. But that didn't wind up in the episode ("After The Fall") that aired.

"We believe we have landed the brightest rising coaching star in college football today. We're looking forward to a long and prosperous relationship."

—— Texas Tech athletic director Gerald Myers, introducing Leach as the new Red Raiders football coach, 1999

"IT'S A GOOD IDEA TO SHAVE FOR TV GAMES."

—— Leach, on his game-day appearance

"I'm amazed by him. He's like a mad scientist, and I don't mean that in a derogatory fashion. He's not afraid to try anything, and he has a success rate that amazes me. He's eccentric, and I'm not sure he works at it. He is what he is, and that's the way it is."

—— Former Texas Tech coach Spike Dykes, on Leach, Houston Chronicle, Oct. 31, 2008

"We flew into Orlando and drove to Key West to recruit this kicker and listened to Jimmy Buffet the whole way. Buffet was always singing about pirates; that's where the pirate thing comes from."

—— Hal Mumme, recalling a recruiting trip when he was head coach at Iowa Wesleyan and Leach was an assistant on the staff

"PIRATES FUNCTION AS A TEAM. THERE WERE A LOT OF CASTES AND CLASSES IN ENGLAND AT THE TIME. BUT WITH PIRATES, IT DIDN'T MATTER IF YOU WERE BLACK, WHITE, RICH OR POOR. THE OBJECT WAS TO GET A TREASURE. IF THE CAPTAIN DID A BAD JOB, YOU COULD JUST OVERTHROW HIM."

—— Leach

"Law school was different than undergrad, where you have a lot of fun because there are gorgeous girls running around and you can take all kinds of courses. In undergrad, if I didn't like a particular course,

171

I'd just find something else. But law school was all law, all the time, and everyone there was pretty competitive."

— Leach, recalling his days in law school

"We played in kind of a celebratory fashion, which is really disturbing to me. At some point, we're going to have to purge that if we're going to improve as a football team."

— Leach, after beating Texas A&M on a last-minute touchdown in College Station

"The plan was to squib-kick it to a fat guy. Of course the fat guys at Texas are nimble, and they have good hands."

— Leach, after two penalties had Tech kicking off from its own 8-yard line with one second to play and holding a 1-point lead, 2008

"THAT'S WHY YOU HAVE PRACTICE. IT'S LIKE CHURCHES. YOU HAVE CHURCHES FOR PEOPLE THAT SIN. YOU HAVE PRACTICE FOR PEOPLE THAT AREN'T PERFECT PLAYERS."

— Leach, on a freshman's inconsistent performance in practice

"We don't have any alibis for injuries. Teams that sit and talk about injuries all the time provide themselves with an excuse for not being successful or as successful as they might. We are not going to provide that for anybody — excuses or alibis for underachievement — so that is another reason (injuries are not mentioned). The other reason, I am not interested in a guy all of a sudden that generates attention just because he is injured. And then the other thing, well I just think it's journalism at its lowest level."

— Leach, on his policy of not discussing injuries with the media

"He says that if just anybody could play quarterback in this system, he'd recruit a girl from the Swedish Bikini Team because she'd be a lot more fun to watch."

— Texas Tech quarterback Cody Hodges, on Leach's offensive system

"HE HAD THAT WHOLE JOHN WAYNE QUALITY. THE ULTIMATE DUST AND TUMBLEWEEDS COMING FROM ABILENE, QUIET KIND OF GUY. EVEN NOW HE KIND OF IS."

— Leach, on quarterback Taylor Potts of Abilene

"It wasn't one of those deals where you're introducing him to pretty girls and taking him for a steak dinner. I didn't have a lot of furniture in my office, so we basically sat cross-legged on the floor watching video and talking until he said he'd rather be a Sooner than go to Utah State."

— Leach, on recruiting quarterback Josh Heupel when Leach was offensive coordinator at Oklahoma

"I'M NOT A BIG SCIENCE FICTION GUY, BUT I THINK THAT EVERYBODY WAS SURPRISED THAT THERE WAS FINALLY A GOOD STAR TREK MOVIE. IT WAS MORE LIKE THE (TV) SERIES. SADLY, MOST OF THOSE STAR TREK MOVIES HAVE BEEN WORSE THAN AN EPISODE OF THE ORIGINAL SERIES. THIS STAR TREK, BY FAR, HANDS DOWN, NO HOLDS BARRED, IS THE BEST STAR TREK MOVIE THAT THEY'VE HAD IN YEARS. ...I SAW "INGLOURIOUS BASTERDS," WHICH I THOUGHT WAS DECENT. I THOUGHT THAT THE ANTICIPATION WAS GREAT, DIDN'T THINK THE PAYOFF WAS AS GOOD AS YOU'RE TYPICALLY USED TO IN A QUENTIN TARANTINO MOVIE. EVEN THOUGH THIS WAS WORTH SEEING, I THOUGHT THE OTHER ONES WERE BETTER. I THOUGHT "JACKIE BROWN" WAS BETTER. I THOUGHT "PULP FICTION" WAS BETTER. THEN, OF COURSE, THE EARLY ONES — YOU KNOW HE WROTE "TRUE ROMANCE," WHICH IS AWESOME. AND THEN "RESERVOIR DOGS," WHICH IS A BETTER MOVIE."

— Leach, offering his summer movie reviews to the media, 2009

"Everybody's all surprised every time this stuff happens. It surprises me everybody gets surprised, because it happens every year like this that there are surprises. The most surprising thing would be if there weren't any surprises. So therefore, in the final analysis, none of it's really that sur-prising."

— Leach, on upsets

"I'VE ONLY BEEN TO PHILLY a COUPLE OF TIMES BE-FORE — I'VE ALWAYS LIKED IT FROM a DISTANCE. I ALWAYS WONDERED WHY THAT WAS. WAS IT THE GOOD FOOD, I'M THINKING, YES, IT'S GOOD FOOD, BUT THAT'S NOT EXACTLY IT_ IF THE FANS DON'T LIKE THE WAY THINGS ARE GOING FOOTBALL-WISE THEY THROW SNOWBALLS, WHICH I LIKE, BECAUSE I THINK FANS SHOULD BE INVOLVED IN THE GAME AND SHOULD HAVE A LITTLE BIT OF PASSION IN REGARD TO WHAT'S GOING ON."

— Leach, in his acceptance speech for the George Munger Coach of the Year award presented by the Maxwell Football Club in Philadelphia, 2008

"Occasionally a player gets into some kind of bind and I have ideas, but mostly I use it to get out of jury duty."

— Leach, when asked if he uses his law degree in coaching

"When he starts commenting about players of mine, that bothered me a little bit – (Stephen) McGee and that whole thing. He likes the rivalry. I think he liked the idea that he could get Aggies' goats when he wanted to...I enjoyed playing those games, yeah."

— Texas A&M coach Mike Sherman, recalling the Texas A&M–Texas Tech rivalry with Leach

174

"I'm not into hocus-pocus, but there's something to this."
—— Leach, on the New Age movement

"TIMEOUTS ARE A LITTLE BIT LIKE MONEY. YOU DON'T WANT TO DIE WITH THEM AND GIVE THEM TO YOUR KIDS. SO YOU MIGHT AS WELL USE THEM IF YOU NEED THEM."
—— Leach, doing TV commentary on the North Carolina State–Central Florida game, 2010

"There's very little salad at Cagle's (steakhouse), so the girl will be forced to eat in front of you, which is something that women hate. But if you can make them do it, the earlier the better. The more they'll conversate and show their true self. I'm a big movie guy, if you want to do more like I did when I was your age you can go to the Stars and Stripes drive-in theater because that's what they had in Cody, Wyoming. But then you want to end it somewhere like some cool coffee shop type of place. Where there's bizarre looking characters going in and out. So if the conversation isn't going well, you can reference some of the characters you see coming and going from the place. And then, if it's a huge night and you're really having a good time, then you can trade computer schemes. And e-mails and all that mischief people are up to nowadays which I know nothing about."
—— Leach, offering dating advice to a college freshman

"That's kind of been a constipated effort there by UCF."
—— Leach, during the North Carolina State–University of Central Florida telecast

"I'M NOT A BIG PICTURE GUY. I LIVE IN THE MOMENT."
—— Leach

Bibliography / Further Reading

Books

Abel, Bob and Michael Valenti. *Sports Quotes: The Insiders' View of the Sports World.* New York: Facts on File, 1983.

Adler, Bill. *Baseball Wit.* New York: Crown, 1986.

Adler, Bill and Bill Adler, Jr. *Ross Perot – An American Maverick Speaks Out.* New York: Citadel Press, 1994.

Blair, Sam. *Earl Campbell – The Driving Force.* Waco: Word Press. 1980.

Bohls, Kirk and John Maher. *Bleeding Orange: Trouble and Triumph Deep in the Heart of Texas Football.* New York: St. Martin's, 1991.

Bosworth, Brian with Rick Reilly. *The Boz.* New York: Charter Books, 1989.

Bouton, Jim. *I'm Glad You Didn't Take It Personally.* New York: Dell, 1971.

Burton, Alan. *'Til the Fat Lady Sings: Classic Texas Sports Quotes.* Lubbock: Texas Tech University Press, 1994.

Burton, Alan. *Dallas Cowboys: Quips and Quotes.* Abilene: State House Press, 2006.

Chieger, Bob. *Voices of Baseball: Quotations on the Summer Game.* New York: Signet, 1983.

Chieger, Bob and Pat Sullivan. *Football's Greatest Quotes.* New York: Simon and Schuster, 1990.

Chieger, Bob and Pat Sullivan. *Inside Golf.* New York: Atheneum, 1985.

Dickson, Paul. *Baseball's Greatest Quotations.* New York: Harper Collins, 1991.

Dykes, Spike with Dave Boling. *Tales from the Texas Tech Sideline.* Champagne, IL: Sports Publishing, 2004.

Davis, Creath. *The Team With Heart: Highland Park Football '84 Scots.* Palm Desert, CA: Person to Person Books, 1985.

Feinstein, John. *A Good Walk Spoiled.* Boston: Little, Brown, 1995.

Freeman, Criswell. *The Golfer's Book of Wisdom.* Nashville, TN: Walnut Grove Press, 1995.

Fry, Hayden with George Wine. *A High Porch Picnic.* Champagne, IL: Sports Publishing,

Garrison, Walt with John Tullius. *Once A Cowboy.* New York: Random House, 1988.

Glanville, Jerry and J. David Miller. *Elvis Don't Like Football.* New York: MacMillan, 1990.

Green, Lee. *Sportswit.* New York: Ballantine, 1984.

Gregston, Gene. *Hogan: The Man Who Played for Glory.* Grass Valley, CA: The Book Legger, 1986.

Heard, Robert. *You Scored One More Point Than A Dead Man: The Irresistible, Sardonic Humor of Abe Lemons.* Austin: Lemons-Heard, 1978.

Heard, Robert. *Dance With Who Brung Us: Quips and Quotes from Darrell Royal.* Austin: Jenkins, 1976.

Kaplan, David and Daniel Griffin. *The Best of Bum: The Quotable Bum Phillips.* Austin: Texas Monthly Press, 1980.

Layne, Bobby with Bob Drum. *Always On Sunday.* Englewood Cliffs, NJ: Prentice-Hall, 1962.

Mercer, Bill. *Play by Play: Tales from a Sports Broadcasting Insider.* Lanham: Taylor Trade, 2007.

Miller, Norm. *To all my fans...from Norm Who?*, Houston: Double Play, 2009.

Nelson, Kevin. *Baseball's Greatest Quotes.* New York: Simon and Schuster, 1982.

Parietti, Jeff. *The Book of Truly Stupid Sports Quotes.* New York: Harper Collins, 1986.

Pennington, Richard. *For Texas I Will: The History of Memorial Stadium.* Austin: Historical Publications, 1992.

Phillips, Bum and Ray Buck. *He Ain't No Bum.* Virginia Beach: Jordan, 1979.

Plaut, David. *Speaking of Baseball.* Philadelphia: Running Press, 1993.

Postman, Andrew and Larry Stone. *Ultimate Book of Sports Lists.* New York: Bantam.

Reid, Jan. *Vain Glory.* Fredericksburg, TX: Shearer, 1986.

Royal, Darrell with Blackie Sherrod. *Darrell Royal Talks Football.* Englewood Cliffs, NJ: Prentice-Hall, 1963.

Sampson, Curt. *Hogan.* Nashville, TN: Rutledge Hill Press, 1996.

Schaap, Dick. *The Masters: The Winning of a Golf Classic.* New York: Random House, 1971.

Schoor, Gene. *Billy Martin — The Story of Baseball's Unpredictable Genius.* Garden City, NY: Doubleday, 1980.

Sports Illustrated. *They Said It!* New York: Oxmoor House, 1990.

St. John, Bob. *Heart of a Lion, The Wild and Woolly Life of Bobby Layne.* Dallas: Taylor Publishing, 1991.

Stowers, Carlton. *Friday Night Heroes: A Look at Texas High School Football.* Austin: Eakin Press, 1983.

Tips, Kern. *Football — Texas Style: An Illustrated History of the Southwest Conference.* Garden City: Doubleday, 1964.

Trevino, Lee and Sam Blair. *They Call Me Super Mex.* New York: Random House, 1982.

Woy, Bucky with Jack Patterson. *Sign 'Em Up, Bucky: The Adventures of a Sports Agent.* New York: Hawthorn Books, 1975.

Magazines

D Magazine
Dallas Life Magazine
Golf Digest
Golf Week
Inside the Astrodome
Longhorn Sports
Newsweek
The North Texan (University of North Texas)
Parade Magazine
Scene Magazine
The Sporting News
Sports Illustrated
Sport Magazine
Texas Football
Texas Lawyer
Texas Monthly
Texas Sports
Texas Sportsworld
Time

Newspapers

Austin American-Statesman
Colorado Springs Gazette
Dallas Morning News
Dallas Times Herald
Denver Post
Fort Worth Star-Telegram
Herald Democrat
Houston Chronicle
Louisville Courier-Gazette
Louisville Courier-Journal
Lubbock Avalanche-Journal

Miami Herald
New York Times
The Oklahoman
San Antonio Express-News
San Francisco Chronicle
San Francisco Examiner
San Jose Mercury News
Sherman Democrat
Texas Techsan
The Daily Toreador (Texas Tech)
The University Daily (Texas Tech)
USA Today
Waco Tribune Herald
Wichita Falls Record News

Websites

astros.com
doubletnation.com
pgatour.com
redraiders.com
texastech.com
yahoosports.com

Radio

Houston Astros Game Broadcasts
Humble-Enco-Exxon Football Broadcasts
Texas Tech Radio Post-Game Interview
The Ticket
WBAP-Fort Worth

Television

ABC Monday Night Football
CBS 60 Minutes
KAMC-Lubbock

ESPN
Fox Southwest College Football TV Show
Fox Sports Post-Game Interview
The Abe Lemons Show
NBC Tonight Show
WFAA-Dallas

Movies

Friday Night Lights

Media Guides

Texas Tech Football
University of Texas Football
University of Texas Basketball

Newsletters

Robert Heard's Inside Texas

News Services

Associated Press

Acknowledgments

Many thanks go to my wife Michelle for her patience and time in assisting with the editing of this manuscript. Also thanks to my daughter Katie, who in addition to being a knowledgeable sports fan, is a bright and talented young woman headed to college. Kudos also go out to my illustrator, Rick Atkinson, for contributing his artistic talents and editing suggestions. I also want to recognize Jim Rogers and Randy Cummings at Zone Press for all of their assistance. Another word of thanks goes to Eddie Thompson, a retired Texas high school coach who read the manuscript and followed up with some recommendations.

Three friends from years ago deserve mention for their influence and encouragement in past endeavors:

- *The late Jack Blunk, who, as my first grade Methodist Sunday School teacher, preached the gospel of John Wesley and Darrell Royal.*
- *The late Jessica Russell, a journalism teacher who advised me to pursue a writing career.*
- *Former basketball coach Tim Williams, who made me realize that most people skim over a game story to just read the quotes!*

I would like to thank attorney and friend Tom Akins of Denison. And finally, a very special thanks to Mike Leach for writing the Foreword.

OTHER BOOKS BY ALAN BURTON

"til the fat lady sings"
Classic Texas Sports Quotes
Texas Tech University Press (1994)

"rave on"
Classic Texas Music Quotes
Texas Tech University Press (1996)

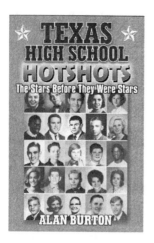

Texas High School Hotshots:
The Stars Before They Were Stars
Republic of Texas Press (2002)

Dallas Cowboys Quips and Quotes
State House Press (2006)

About the Author

Alan Burton is Director of University Communications at Southeastern Oklahoma State University in Durant, Oklahoma. His 25-year career in the PR/communications field includes stints as sports editor of the *Sherman Democrat* and Director of Community Relations for the Sherman (Texas) Independent School District. Burton has earned writing awards from the Associated Press, Texas School Public Relations Association, and the Oklahoma College Public Relations Association. He is a graduate of Sherman High School and Texas Tech University, where he earned a B.A. in English. A native of Sherman, Burton and his wife, Michelle, a high school counselor, reside in Denison, Texas, with their daughter Katie. In addition to *Pirates, Soldiers & Fat Little Girlfriends*, Burton is the author of four other books: *'til the fat lady sings — Classic Texas Sports Quotes*; *rave on – Classic Texas Sports Quotes*; *Texas High School Hotshots – The Stars Before They Were Stars*; and *Dallas Cowboys Quips and Quotes*.

About the Illustrator

Rick Atkinson is a writer and editorial cartoonist based in McKinney, Texas. His stories have been featured in newspapers across Texas, including Sherman, Midland, Wylie, Port Arthur and Borger. Atkinson has covered high school football for *The Dallas Morning News* since 2002. His SMU football and men's basketball stories appear on cusa-fans.com. Atkinson's cartoons have been featured in Sherman-Denison's *Herald Democrat* newspaper, as well as SMU's *Daily Campus* and *The Wylie News*. His artwork is now featured on theheckler.com/dallas. Atkinson is a graduate of Sherman High School and Southern Methodist University, where he received a B.A. in Psychology and was a member of the SMU Mustang Band. After college, Atkinson was an officer in the U.S. Marine Corps for 10 years, serving as a helicopter pilot in Kaneohe Bay, Hawaii, and later as a fixed-wing instructor pilot at Naval Air Station Corpus Christi, Texas. He was a pilot for American Airlines for 13 years. Atkinson is married to the former Debbie Spiecher of Lufkin, Texas.

Index

CPSIA information can be obtained at www.ICGtesting.com
Printed in the USA
LVOW081744091211

258670LV00007B/150/P